WALKING IN ESSEX

About the Author

Peter Aylmer's rich understanding of the Essex countryside started young, visiting his uncle's farm in the Rodings. Since discovering walking as a pastime when a young man, he's since climbed many hills and walked many long-distance paths all over Britain, but still relishes the surprise on people's faces when he tells them that some of his favourite walking is within his home county; Essex has many hundreds of fine unspoilt miles for walking, and a varied and surprising history to be uncovered.

Peter's website is www.trailman.co.uk.

Other Cicerone guides by the author
Walking in London

WALKING IN ESSEX

25 WALKS AND A 96 MILE 'ACROSS ESSEX' ROUTE

by Peter Aylmer

JUNIPER HOUSE, MURLEY MOSS,
OXENHOLME ROAD, KENDAL, CUMBRIA LA9 7RL
www.cicerone.co.uk

© Peter Aylmer 2019
Second edition 2019
ISBN: 978 1 78631 022 4
First edition 2013
Printed by KHL Printing, Singapore
A catalogue record for this book is available from the British Library.
All photographs are by the author unless otherwise stated.

© Crown copyright 2019 OS PU100012932

Acknowledgements

Fred Matthews and Harry Bitten, of the West Essex Ramblers, laid down in the 1970s and 1980s a long-distance footpath network for the county, which still forms its backbone. It gave me many years of happy exploration, and many of the places and paths I thus discovered feature in this volume.

The author also wishes to thank Simon Taylor at Essex County Council, Mark Iley of the Essex Wildlife Trust, and Tim Harris and Tony Morrison of the Wren Group, which does so much for wildlife and nature in east London. Thanks too to professional photographer Johnnie Pakington, with whom I worked for many years, for his patient help and support. On a personal level, Liz Fox and Dave Travers have been invaluable in walk testing – I thank Dave (alas, no longer with us) also for having had the good sense to have lived in Felixstowe, so that Essex was our natural meeting point for a quarter-century. In particular I thank my wife Barbara, walk tester, photo model and general motivator, all rolled in to one.

Updates to this Guide

While every effort is made by our authors to ensure the accuracy of guidebooks as they go to print, changes can occur during the lifetime of an edition. Any updates that we know of for this guide will be on the Cicerone website (www.cicerone.co.uk/1022/updates), so please check before planning your trip. We also advise that you check information about such things as transport, accommodation and shops locally. Even rights of way can be altered over time. We are always grateful for information about any discrepancies between a guidebook and the facts on the ground, sent by email to updates@cicerone.co.uk or by post to Cicerone, Juniper House, Murley Moss, Oxenholme Road, Kendal LA9 7RL.

Register your book: To sign up to receive free updates, special offers and GPX files where available, register your book at www.cicerone.co.uk.

Front cover: Arkesden, start point of Walk 16

CONTENTS

Route symbols on OS map extracts
(for OS legend see printed OS maps)

 route

alternative route

 start/finish point

 start point

 finish point

alternative start/finish point

◀ route direction

Features on the overview map

——— County/Unitary boundary

 Urban area

Area of Outstanding
Natural Beauty
eg, *Dedham Vale*

On Whitehall Plain in Epping Forest (Across Essex, Stage 1)

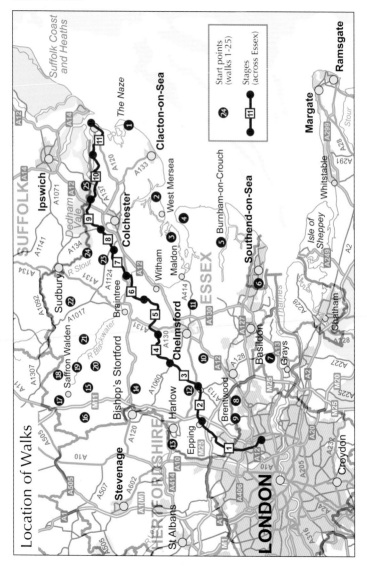

Location of Walks

INTRODUCTION

Green lane before Great Bowsers (Walk 18)

My uncle was a farmer, first in Fyfield, then in Great Easton, so for me going to Essex meant playing with the egg-grading machine or seeing the cows come back for milking, or maybe an evening walk to the village pub. This is still the reality of life for many in the county, and because its population is concentrated in the southern conurbations and a handful of medium-sized towns, there's an awful lot of rural countryside to explore.

I wonder whether any critic of Essex has ever looked at a map. Should they do so, they will see clearly-marked river valleys – culminating in the Area of Outstanding Natural Beauty that is the Stour Valley

– great and ancient forests, and an abundance of green lanes. There are no great heights, it is true, although descend from the 482ft high point near the Hertfordshire border and you will enjoy lovely rolling views across a distant downland landscape.

And then there is the coastline – all Southend, Clacton, tarmacked proms and caravan sites? Well, there are a few, and no reason why not. But at 560 miles, there is a lot of loneliness in between, with saltmarsh raising fine lamb, creeks overwintering internationally-significant bird populations, and a constant alternation between estuary and seashore without parallel throughout these islands.

On Orsett Fen (Walk 7)

Little of south-east England can lay a claim to remoteness; but walk 14 miles south from St Peter's Chapel and you will pass neither habitation nor public road – it requires some skill to better that, even in a national park.

Contemporary authors such as Robert Macfarlane and Jules Pretty are among those who have written about the 'wildness' of Essex. They do so from the viewpoint that the county is a county in flux, and this for me is the heart of the matter. So, for example, Macfarlane visits Rainham Marshes, and discovers how land 'ripe with sewage reek, the groundwater rancid with chemicals' has in ten years been transformed by the RSPB into a place with 'an extraordinary spring soundscape – the sedge and reed warblers chirruping away like gossipy neighbours, the coots squabbling and above all these marsh frogs which make such a belching chorus in the background'. The refreshment of these marshes is by no means unique – on a smaller scale, a similar transformation occurred earlier on Two Tree Island, passed on Walk 6.

Against that you have of course the pressure of population growth, increasingly lax planning laws and climate change. Occasional victories, such as the abandonment of the second runway proposal at Stansted, mean that treasures such as Thaxted (Walk 20) can still be enjoyed in relative peace. I have walked the Essex coast with a trusty 1992 Landranger map which is in places hopelessly inadequate, so frequent are the sea wall breaches that have created new tidal saltmarsh. (Walk 2 and Walk 3 have examples.)

THE GEOLOGY OF ESSEX

A definition first of all: in this book, 'Essex' means the historic county including the London boroughs east of the Lea, roughly equivalent to the post-Roman Kingdom of the East Saxons. Water, important then as now to the defender of a contested territory, defines most of its boundaries: the North Sea to the east, the Thames to the south, the Lea and Stort to the west, and the Stour to the north. Each of these has a character very different to the others, and this one fact alone gives a variety to the landscape.

It's only in the north-west of the county that water-boundaries are absent. Here, the county takes in the catchment area of the upper Cam, and indeed comes within seven miles of Cambridge itself. It's also here that the underpinning geology is of Upper Chalk beds, rather than the London Clay that predominates elsewhere in the county. While never quite emulating the downland scarps of Sussex or Bedfordshire, this chalk country has a distinctive feel of its own, quite literally in terms of the texture under foot, and visually with its undulations and whiteness.

The chalk never disappears from underneath Essex: it dips deep underground, perhaps 400ft below, and reappears in the far south around Grays. The little nature reserve at Chafford Gorges, an easy stroll from Lakeside shopping centre should you tire of retail therapy, is set amid old chalk quarries.

In the basin of London Clay between the two chalk ridges,

The River Colne below Bacon's Farm (Across Essex, Stage 7)

the Thames once flowed. Around 500,000 years ago, the Thames was a tributary of the Rhine, taking a course across the county to roughly where the Blackwater Estuary is now. An effective southern barrier to the river was provided by a mix of sand, clay and flint known as the 'Bagshot Beds', which still emerges at many of the high points in the south of the county including High Beach in Epping Forest and the Danbury Ridge.

The Ice Ages since, which saw ice sheets as far south as Hornchurch, successively pushed the river south, eventually to its present course. But those Ice Ages did far more than divert the Thames. As the ice sheets repeatedly pushed south and retreated north, they scoured the land-surface, dragging materials from elsewhere and uncovering new deposits.

In much of northern Essex, the newer Boulder Clay (perhaps 80,000 years old) overlays London Clay. The two are sufficiently different to affect the agricultural uses of the county: the former has enough chalk and lime bundled within it to be good for crop growing, whereas sheep and cattle thrive on the latter. And where the London Clay silts are deposited around the shoreline, oysters thrive, and flocks of gulls and waders pick out the nutrients from plants and insects.

To return to the rivers of Essex: some define its boundaries, but others define its interior. Between the Thames and Stour estuaries, three other great inlets march into Essex:

the Crouch, the Blackwater and the Colne. Each is the outflow to a river of that name. So effective are the boundary-rivers in constricting Essex that these three interior rivers stray into no other county.

Woodland

After the Ice Ages, much of Essex became heavily wooded – enough to merit its own name in the literature of the prehistoric, the Great Forest of Essex. Early settlers set about clearing the trees where they could, but sufficient remained in medieval times that Henry I could decree that much of the county be set aside as a royal hunting

Hornbeam pollard in Hainault Forest (Walk 9)

Bluebells in Chalkney Wood (Walk 23)

forest. The remnants of this can be seen to this day at Hatfield Forest, where deer were introduced around 1100 to aid the process. The ancient tree-management practices of coppicing and pollarding have been carried out here and elsewhere for many centuries, with the former in particular still a mainstay of woodland management in the county.

Oliver Rackham, that most perceptive writer on English woodlands, pointed to four principal forest-zones in the ancient county. Hatfield, Epping, Hainault and Writtle, the four great surviving forests, lie in a zone that was principally hornbeam. In the chalk of the north-west, ash, maple and hazel predominated. The Stour and Colne valleys supported lime, while further south chestnut predominated. Echoes of that former pattern remain: for example, the small-leaved limes of Chalkney Wood (Walk 23) are now of national importance.

Such has been the pressure on woodlands – particularly marked in Essex, for its lack of stone has led to wood becoming a building material of choice even for churches – that today only six per cent (albeit growing) of the county is wooded. Sweet chestnut, beech and hawthorn are among other prominent species, with willow and alder on river-courses. The elm has made a modest comeback since the depredations of Dutch Elm disease: let's hope that any devastation from ash die-back disease will be localised and temporary rather than widespread and permanent.

Arable land

Although many woodlands are essentially islands within arable lands, this is particularly so in the plateaus between river-valleys – what one might term the Essex tablelands. Here most notably, contemporary management techniques require large field sizes and chemical treatment to produce the crop yields that buyers require. Happily, the worst excesses of pesticide use have been outlawed since the 1970s, and from 2005 environmental stewardship schemes have led to new woods and hedgerows being planted and buffer strips introduced. Between them, these have enabled much wildlife to return, in particular the buzzard and white admiral butterfly in the skies and the otter in the rivers. There are more deer in the county than at any time in recent history; not altogether a positive, for so high are the numbers in some areas, that they are a significant threat to ground flora. Essex woods have long been notable for their bluebells and, on the Suffolk-Cambridgeshire border, their oxlips: pick the right part of spring, and both will present a beautiful spectacle.

Walk the paths in this book and you will get to know Essex hedgerows and field headlands very well. These essential wildlife corridors, linking woodlands and other habitats, enable pollination and develop their own little ecology. As the seasons change, you will see snowdrop, cowslip, forget-me-not, poppy (the county flower), cow parsley, old man's beard and many more. Green lanes are different again: many of them, especially those on the first third of the Essex Way, are all but natural tunnels for

The horse-chestnut avenue north of Duddenhoe End (Walk 16)

lengthy stretches, with little light penetrating the canopy. This makes for cool, if damp underfoot, walking at the height of summer.

All of this might help dispel the stereotype that Essex is either conurbation or prairie farm. They exist, and undoubtedly the grubbing out of hedgerows in the last half of the 20th century led to the loss of much biodiversity as well as, in some areas, the pleasing patchwork that field-patterns can give to the eye. No doubt we enjoy cheaper food as a result. That's the key really: field sizes aren't chosen for their aesthetic impact, but because they are efficient for the farming methods of the day.

The feudal system of the Middle Ages had each peasant tending several small strips of land spread across the lord's estate, strips separated from each other by banks of unploughed turf. Hedgerows every few yards, or even fences, would have been both expensive and inefficient, and restricted to larger-scale boundaries, such as between estates or parishes; these in turn would have been relatively untouched since the Norman conquest, if not Saxon times or before. Indeed, many of these remain.

What folk-memory retains as quintessential English landscape results from the enclosure of land, principally brought in by parliamentary acts from the late 18th century, as landowners moved to restrict common access to the land they owned. As it happens, in Essex this process began far earlier, from Tudor times. (Around a quarter of the present 10,000 miles of hedgerows in Essex are Tudor or earlier.) The great exceptions were around Great Chesterford, where the chalkland fields remained fully open to 1804, and Epping and Hainault forests, the first a victory, the second largely a defeat for the 19th-century anti-enclosure movement. But even in the Essex tablelands, the relics of field patterns remain, and footpaths often follow them.

Coast

Inland Essex is many habitats: coastal Essex gives many more. The holiday-maker knows the sand (yet there isn't much beyond Clacton-to-Walton), and the shingle of Southend, but the bathing requirements of *Homo sapiens* are of little significance compared to the international role of the county's coast for bird life. One acre in every ten of this nation's saltmarsh is in Essex – look out for the blooming of the sea lavender in July; the tidal mud-flats of the river creeks and estuaries wind for miles inland; and cockle banks arise at almost every turn from river to sea. Marshland behind the sea walls – raised mostly from around 1600, but in some areas from the passing of the 'Law of the Marsh' in 1210 – can hide little lagoons, and every borrow-dyke (created by excavation on the landward side of the sea wall) has its reed-bed.

Within these and other coastal habitats, the Darwinian richness of life remains in profusion, each species adapted to its niche, and sometimes adapting to new niches following human intervention. Flocks of brent geese fly 2500 miles to escape the Siberian winter, while waders such as the bar-tailed godwit fly in from Scandinavia. The whimbrel rests here on its migration. Little egrets are increasingly common, and the Dengie Peninsula forms one of the last refuges of the corn bunting. Coastal areas are rich in reptile life too: apart from populations in Danbury and Epping Forest, almost all of the county's adder population is to be found here.

TOWN AND VILLAGE

As well as its relative clay-based geological unity, Essex has had an administrative unity too, stretching back nearly 1600 years to the founding of the kingdom of the East Saxons and formalised in Norman times as the historic county. The splitting away of the east London boroughs in 1965, and Thurrock and Southend in 1998, whatever demographic sense it might have had, counts for naught in this respect.

But there has never been visual unity, at the level of town or village. Many regions of England are distinct because of their harmonious use of a particular stone – perhaps the honeyed limestone of the Cotswolds is the best example, but also the flints of chalky Sussex and the granite of Aberdeen. There is practically no building stone in Essex, so pervasive is the underlying clay: a bit of puddingstone dragged here by glaciers, a few Roman imports left behind, some ragstone shipped across the Thames from Kent, and indeed some flints in the chalklands. Instead, the people of Essex had to improvise as they set about building places in which to live, trade, store grain and worship, and they did so with great inventiveness.

Wood of course was readily available, and ancient buildings great and small survive in it, from grain barns to the roofs, towers and porches of churches throughout the county. Exposed timbers still front many farms and town houses, often from Tudor times, yet barely ever succumbing to chocolate-box tweeness. Near the coast particularly, but liable to crop up almost anywhere, weatherboarding (particularly from the 18th century) provides secure protection from rain.

Wattle-and-daub, and later plaster, filled the gaps between wooden frames; and on the surface of the plaster, to lend decoration, the art of pargetting (patterned plaster in relief) was – still is – pursued. It lends variety to any number of buildings, new as well as old, from simple geometric shapes to complex tessellations, from the wildlife of farm and field to scenes of rural life. The Romans used brick wherever they went, and here clay soils are a positive benefit. Their successors lost the art though; in England, it took Essex workers to re-discover it, in 12th-century Coggeshall. Soon, it too was infilling and, before long, providing the sole structure for some of the great houses of the county.

Roofing was once largely, and often still is, of thatch: the village of Arkesden and its surroundings still have enough properties to keep two local firms busy.

Most towns have expanded rapidly and are still doing so, Chelmsford increasing from 5513 in 1863 to over 157,000 in 2011 and becoming the county's only city the year after. But many of the villages you will walk through with this book have populations similar to those many hundreds of years ago. The 792 of Ashdon today is not too different to the 670 estimated for 1547; Castle Hedingham had 1052 in 1818, 1000 now. With smaller family units nowadays, they are housed in many more dwellings, bringing infilling that can be a blight if not sensitively handled. In Essex particularly, where church and manor house are often separate from the village proper (see Across Essex, Stage 8), it's easy to fall into the trap of assuming that these two buildings form the soul of the village, while for many villagers they will have represented simply seats of power to which they had to give weekly, or perhaps less frequent, obedience, be it spiritual or temporal, otherwise remote (not only physically) from their everyday lives.

That said, the Essex church is an excellent place to get some grip on the history of the area you are walking in. Almost all of those passed in

Great Bardfield (Walk 21)

this guide keep open doors. Where you can, go in. They are usually well-placed for a break. They may surprise you with wall-paintings, wood carving or elaborate ceilings. They can tell you much, simply by looking around: are there dominant families, honoured by memorials on walls or in church-yards? Is there any effort to commemorate the honest toil of Gray's village-Hampdens or mute inglorious Miltons? What does the record of rectors, perhaps dating back to before the Conquest, show – successive deaths in plague centuries perhaps, turmoil as the nation swung from Catholic to Protestant, back again, then rent by civil war and Puritan ascendancy? Is there modern retrenchment, as church livings are combined in team ministries? As you consider all this, whether

of religious faith or not, a coin or two in the church box will be a small price to pay for such an exploration of this county, its country, its buildings and its people.

WHEN TO GO

Spring is a wonderful time in Essex, with its bluebell and oxlip woods at their best – but the autumn colours can be spectacular too, and summer hedgerows bring new flowers to the fore. Don't discount the first chills of winter either, especially on the coast, where flocks of migrant birds arrive from Scandinavia and Siberia to escape the sharp cold of those northern lands. That might surprise us human beings – an easterly wind whipping off the North Sea can be a bitter experience

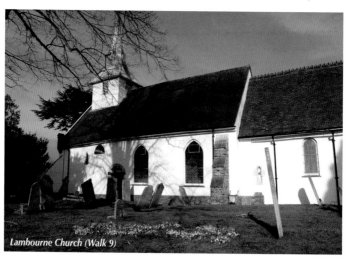

Lambourne Church (Walk 9)

The Colne in flood at Chappel (Walk 24)

at any time of year – but as with most of lowland England, there's no reason to avoid any particular season with the right clothing; but do take account of any weather warnings. Prolonged rain is perhaps the most significant hazard: not because of its likelihood – its eastern situation makes Essex one of the driest of counties – but for its effect on the clay soils, which can become especially heavy, as anyone who has taken a direct line across a newly-ploughed field can tell you.

The mid-August RiZE Festival brings tens of thousands of music lovers to Chelmsford every year, which can clog up the local area. Few other events bring such numbers. It's worth searching out some of the appealing local festivals of Essex, such as the Colchester Oyster Fayre and the Thaxted music festival (both early summer), or even smaller-scale happenings such as Morris dancers on a village green, and perhaps arranging a few days of walks around them.

GETTING THERE AND GETTING AROUND

Rural Essex starts just ten miles from central London with Epping Forest. A favourite Saturday treat, when our children were small, was to quickly access the M11 from our home in East Ham, and within half an hour be on a village green with a quiet pub in the Matchings. Essex is a vital lung for many in the crowded inner-city. And it's easy to get to Essex from most parts of Britain, and easy to move around it once you are there.

By train from London, the two main lines both run from Liverpool

Central London across the valley of the Rom (Walk 8)

Street, one in the west of the county on its way to Cambridge (with a spur to Stansted Airport), the other heading north-east through Chelmsford and Colchester to Ipswich and Norwich. Branches serve Southend, Braintree, Sudbury, Clacton, Walton and Harwich. Colchester is an hour from London. Another Southend line runs from Fenchurch Street, through Leigh-on-Sea. Don't forget the Central Line of the tube, which keeps to the Roding Valley, just to the east of Epping Forest, throughout its length – indeed plenty of local trains, buses and tubes serve the London area walks in this book.

From the Midlands and north you can avoid London, using the Stansted Airport service which runs from Birmingham (3hr 15mins) through Leicester, Peterborough (1hr 30mins, connecting to the East Coast main line) and Cambridge, or the useful line which links Peterborough to Ipswich (1hr 45mins), just 20 minutes from Colchester.

If driving, the M25 links to the two main arterial roads, the M11 and A12, each roughly parallel to one of the two main train lines. The A14 from the Midlands and the A1 from the North both feed into the M11. Within the county, roads vary – even some A roads, such as that down the Colne Valley, are reminders of a less rushed past, and country lanes can frequently be single track, but new developments such as the A120 in the middle of the county are built for speed.

By air, the county's airports at Stansted and Southend have scheduled flights from the UK, Europe and beyond as well as rail services onward. Stansted has a coach from the airport to Chelmsford and Southend and buses to Colchester and elsewhere.

Most A roads, and the former A roads replaced by the M11, have decent bus services linking the major towns. Often, these also serve nearby larger villages. That said, there are large parts of the county not easily reached by public transport, and some – including one as close to the capital as Mill Green (Walk 10) – not at all. Further, buses in the evenings and on Sundays are almost non-existent in rural areas, and the dreaded weekend and bank holiday railway engineering works can make the train impractical at these popular times. But if you can use public transport, do – locals will appreciate that you are helping keep their service afloat, there's an undoubted environmental gain, and if your walk does end at a pub, you need have no fear about enjoying what it has to offer.

The Traveline site, www.traveline.info, gives door-to-door public transport routes, and also holds detailed bus timetables – click the 'Timetables' link and enter the name of the town or village you want to go to. Use the National Rail site, www.nationalrail.co.uk, for rail times, or the local operator – at the time of writing, Greater Anglia, www.greateranglia.co.uk.

And if you ride a bike, why not bring it? Essex is a popular county for cycle touring, so you could easily combine cycling and walking.

WHERE TO STAY

Chelmsford, Saffron Walden and Colchester are the principal hubs relevant to the walks in this book, and any would make a fine base for a car-free walking break. (With a car, almost anywhere in the county will serve – perhaps a small town such as Thaxted, or a village near the Colne Valley.) Of the three, Chelmsford is the easiest – its bus station is right next to the train station. Colchester's bus station is not too far from the town train station, but far fewer trains serve this than the principal North station, although some country-bound buses do pass the latter. Saffron Walden is a little distant from the nearest station, Audley End, but with a regular link.

Accommodation options are plentiful in all three of these centres. Check out www.visitessex.com for more information on these and other options.

ACCESS AND WAYMARKING

Waymarking in Essex is generally good. You will get especially used to the distinctive concrete posts that show where many paths leave roads; unique to the county, these are now over 50 years old and are weathering in a surprisingly beautiful way, colonised by mosses and lichens in greens and golds. At path junctions, look for the marker posts, usually no more than 3ft high. Footpaths are usually marked in yellow, and bridleways in blue.

Footpath marker on the Essex Way

The County Council have a five-year programme of walking each path they are responsible for – that is, excluding the London boroughs, Thurrock and Southend-on-Sea – and local walking groups such as the Ramblers are active in reporting any difficulties and trying to resolve that may occur. In Essex, there are very few 'right-to-roam' areas, shown on waymarkers by a brown logo of walker traversing rolling countryside – however, most of Hatfield Forest is covered in this way.

Elsewhere, walkers have the right to traverse rights of way, but not other paths, unless a landowner grants permission. This cuts both ways. If a landowner obstructs a right of way with a fence, for example, you have a perfect right to climb over the fence and continue. You need, of course, to be absolutely certain that you are in the right place. Good landowners – in all honesty, most of them – know this, and therefore take trouble to maintain rights of way. In return, you should be considerate too, most particularly in shutting gates.

One trick worth knowing: if you come to a gate or stile and there's no waymarker, check on its other side. If there's no marker there either, you're probably off line. Another: if you end up crossing barbed wire, you shouldn't be. And one useful tip: often, the directions say 'continue for 100 metres' or similar; these will make more sense if you know how many double paces (right-foot-to-right-foot or the opposite) you generally take over this distance, so find a place where you know the distance

Sea wall sign at The Strood (Walk 2)

Felixstowe on the horizon (Across Essex, Stage 11)

(or use a distance-measuring app) and count your strides. It's likely to be between 55 and 75 per 100 metres.

The biggest difficulty walkers might find is in crossing newly ploughed fields, mostly in late summer and autumn. Usually the farmer leaves a walker's line between planted crops, but before they grow this will not be evident. It's a particular issue on Essex's clay soils – a couple of hundred yards across muddy furrows can make boots feel like lead weights! In circumstances such as these, many walkers will divert around the headland, and it's unlikely a landowner would object to this. Indeed, a few of the walks in this book advise a route that is not a right of way, where there is clear evidence that it is a regularly-walked alternative.

WHAT TO TAKE

Because of the county's clay soils it's strongly advised to wear proper walking boots if you're going to be crossing fields in or after heavy rain, but good walking shoes or trainers can be perfectly adequate or indeed preferable at drier times. The shorter walks need almost nothing in the way of specialist clothing, but if you're out for a long half-day or more, look for a wicking top, trousers (if not shorts) that will dry easily (so not jeans or cords), and something warm to pull on when you stop. If there is any doubt in the forecast at all, take a windproof and/or waterproof layer, preferably made of breathable fabric such as Gore-Tex or Event. The more extreme the weather, the better your gear needs to be.

23

It makes sense to carry your mobile phone in case of emergencies but by no means can you rely on it to get a signal, even in villages. Be prepared to get yourself to the nearest habitation to call for help.

MAPS

The extracts in this book from Ordnance Survey Landranger maps, at 1:50,000 scale, when coupled with the route descriptions, will keep you on track. The county as a whole is covered by sheets 154, 155, 166 to 169, 177 and 178.

There is even more detail on the Explorer series at 1:25,000. For the walker, these are invaluable in showing field boundaries and so help resolve the old question of 'which side of that hedge should I be?' The county is covered by 162, 163, 174 to 176, 183, 184, 195, 196, 209 and 210.

Mapping software allows you to scale Landranger or Explorer maps as you wish and print off specific areas relevant to your walk. Anquet, Quo and Memory Map are three of the best known. All enable maps to be saved to GPS devices, and some to smart-phones; for the latter, ViewRanger is a dedicated app.

USING THIS GUIDE

There should be enough detail in the route descriptions, including the map extracts, to follow each walk without using a separate **printed map**, but it's always good practice to relate the description to the map as you go;

Entering meadows on the River Ter (Across Essex, Stage 5)

The chapel and halfway stone, Coggeshall Abbey (Across Essex, Stage 6)

this will help make sure you don't go wildly off beam, and also guards against any changes in the waymarking: signs can get overgrown in high summer, for example.

More to the point, relating to the map gives you a fuller account of the countryside you are walking through, and not just its shape; the alert map user will spot many details, historic and natural, that the guide can't hope to include. Researching the Danbury walk, for example, I once found myself off-path but following a ditch that seemed to have no purpose as drainage: the map showed it was a parish boundary-marker no doubt dating back many hundreds of years.

On the coastal walks, it's tempting to drop down onto the foreshore if possible, and a couple of walks

explicitly suggest it. If you are particularly keen to do this, **check the tide tables** before you go: the Admiralty website http://easytide.ukho.gov.uk is authoritative. In general, don't stray out, especially on the muddy flats around much of the Essex coast, on an incoming tide, and take care at any time. Indeed there's one wonderful walk – the Broomway off Foulness Island – which is comparable in danger to Morecambe Bay. So easily can the unwary be caught by the tide, that it needs a professional guide for safety.

Each of the stages in the **Across Essex** section is enjoyable in its own right, and between them they span the full variety of the Essex countryside, chalklands excepted. But by design they form a long-distance path, a

25

traverse of Epping Forest followed by the Essex Way. If walking a long route like this is new to you, there are some notes in the introduction to Across Essex to help.

The OS maps required are listed in the **information box** at the start of each of the routes, in addition to the distance, an estimated walking time (a fairly relaxed 4km per hour plus an extra half hour), refreshments available en route and car parking and public transport options. In the route descriptions, a 'minor road' carries very little motor traffic, a rural 'lane' even less but is unmetalled and a 'track' is also unmetalled but less robust. 'Footbridges' have at least one hand rail; 'plank bridges' do not; neither carries motor traffic, and if wooden both are easy to slip off when wet. But what was in place when this volume was researched may change with the course of time; please see the Advice to Readers box at the front of this book and let Cicerone know if you find that this is so.

This book will, I hope, work on two levels. All of the 22 circular and 14 linear routes described here will provide excellent recreation in enjoyable scenery, and so cleanse the mind of everyday pressures: that is certainly my primary purpose, whenever I embark on a walk. But there will be enough information for the alert walker to see the country through which they are passing not simply as a once-and-for-all static 'heritage' but a county which is immeasurably enriched by an understanding of that fourth dimension, time.

The Naze tower from the beach

COAST AND ESTUARY

27

WALK 1

The Naze peninsula

Start/Finish	Walton-on-the-Naze pier (TM 254 215); parking on The Parade and off the High Street
Distance	5½ miles (9km)
Walking time	2½hr
Maps	OS Explorer 184, Landranger 168
Refreshments	Pubs and cafés in the town, and a tearoom in the Naze tower
Public transport	Buses from Colchester (not Sundays) and Clacton; trains from Colchester

There is no better introduction to the Essex coastline than the Naze peninsula. Intricate backwaters host a wide variety of wildlife, and offer a playground for those who crew small boats; and shingle spit and sandy beach form the tide-margins, along with that Essex rarity, the cliff. These cliffs, formed two million years ago from iron-rich but soft Red Crag, are among the most prolific nationally for bird and tree fossils. The grassy top of the peninsula is a complete contrast, and the view from the Naze tower gives a broad panorama of coastal Essex and Suffolk.

With the **pier** on your right, walk slightly uphill for a few yards and turn left along Newgate Street. Follow this past the Victory pub, then turn right along the High Street, and left into North Street. At the end, turn right onto the sea wall, behind houses.

> The marshland immediately adjacent was once a millpond, and later a boating lake known as **The Mere**, which closed in 1976.

Keep on the sea wall for the next three miles; the only possible point of doubt is early on, after the holiday park, where you need to go straight past the entrance to a small boatyard. Ahead, the cranes of the vast port of Felixstowe, across the Stour estuary, come ever closer but never intrude.

The cliffs below the Naze

THE NAZE

WALTON-
ON-THE-NAZE

WALTON BACKWATERS

Beyond the boatyard, where a channel quaintly known as The Twizzle branches off the Walton channel, you enter the area known as the Walton backwaters. Here, a mixture of low-lying islands, tidal saltmarshes, mud flats and sand flats provides a safe haven for many overwintering birds, including redshank, shelduck and teal, and a colony of several dozen harbour and grey seals – russet-coloured rather than grey, owing to the iron in the Red Crag.

Of the islands, Skipper's Island is accessible by foot causeway with permission from Essex Wildlife Trust; if you see a Land Rover apparently crossing low-tide mud, it's on the longer causeway to Horsey Island, which has a bloodstock farm. The Backwaters were the setting for *Secret Water*, the eighth in the Swallows and Amazons series of children's novels by Arthur Ransome.

The foreshore is a low tide alternative, following it from the interpretation board to the steps up to the Crag Walk.

There's a slight change of character at the right turn onto Cormorant Creek (TM 250 248). It's clear now that you are heading towards the open sea; it would seem logical that the creek gives access to it, but in fact it's barred by a shingle spit topped by low sand dunes and a shell bank. At the closest point to the foreshore, by a Hamford Water interpretation board, the walk turns right again. ◄ Pass a couple of small lagoons on an asphalt path, and the effect of erosion becomes immediately obvious: within a few yards, the path simply disappears.

Do not attempt to cross the fence. Keep beside it, follow the first grass path left into shrubs and out to the grassy plateau, and continue ahead to the **Naze Tower**. The tower, 86ft high, was built in 1720 to aid shipping. It now houses a tearoom, art gallery and viewing platform. Continue down the steps by an information board just past the café.

The cliffs are **eroding** by up to 2m a year; the medieval village of Walton is now several miles out to sea. For a more recent example of what erosion can do, note that the Second World War pillboxes on the foreshore once lay above the cliffs. It's worth taking the Crag Walk, constructed in 2011, for a close-up view of the eroding cliffs. The Walk also helps to protect the land on which the tower sits, but such is the power of the sea that no attempt is being made to protect the northern end of the peninsula.

Continue from the bottom of the steps past the beach huts – or if you can, on the sand, dabbling your toes. On your way, the old lifeboat house hosts the Walton Maritime Museum. Finally, keep along the esplanade back to the pier.

The Naze Tower

WALK 2
Mersea Island

Start/Finish	Cudmore Grove Country Park (TM 064 145)
Distance	13½ miles (22km) or 5½ miles (9km)
Walking time	6hr; 2½hr for the shorter route
Maps	OS Explorer 184, Landranger 168
Refreshments	At the start; in West Mersea, pubs, cafés and seafood bars; Mersea Island vineyard café; on the shorter walk, Dog and Pheasant pub
Public transport	(For the longer walk) bus from Colchester (not Sundays), and start at either The Strood or West Mersea

Of all the small islands of Britain, Mersea would be the best for a food-lover to be marooned on. This most easterly English island has its own vineyard and brewery; its saltmarshes deliver tangy samphire, and fatten lamb for the best London butchers; and from its pure sea waters come scallop, crab and lobster, and oysters that grace the tables of some of the finest restaurants of Europe. Yet time your visit carefully, or you may have a late return if the tidal causeway of The Strood is under water.

Both walks start from the information room at the **Cudmore Grove Country Park**. Follow the sign to the beach, keeping the trees on your right, and joining the coast at the entry to the East Mersea Flats National Nature Reserve. Stay on the surfaced path. Ahead, across the Colne Estuary, is Brightlingsea, with the Victorian folly of Bateman's (leaning) **Tower** in front. At the steps, the walk turns from sea to estuary, and with it comes an immediate change in tone: from the lapping – or, sometimes, crashing – of sea against shingle, to the pre-dominance of bird-chatter that characterises estuarine Essex. ◄ Keep along the sea wall, now grass-topped, past the Colchester Oyster Fishery, whose oyster beds date back to 1189.

It's possible to walk out onto the shingle spit, and from April to September catch a small ferry that runs to Brightlingsea.

Shorter route

For the shorter walk, veer left off the sea wall just before the second kissing gate from the fishery, to another kissing gate, and keep to the right edge of a field. Go over a plank bridge into a tree-belt and turn left, soon picking up a lane, which veers right and left and becomes a minor road. Turn right past the **Dog and Pheasant** pub, and left at a concrete sign 200 metres further on, keeping a hedge on your left around two sides of a field. Turn left onto a minor road, past **East Mersea Church**. ▷ Continue into Coopers Beach holiday park, rejoining the main walk.

Sabine Baring-Gould, writer of 'Onward Christian Soldiers' and an important folk-song collector, was rector here from 1870 to 1881.

Continue on the sea wall, past the long curve of **Reeveshall Marsh**, one of the prime grazing grounds for Essex salt-marsh lamb. In contrast to this tranquil scene, warning notices guard against landing on the other side of the channel; their marshes are part of the Fingringhoe Ranges, training grounds for the army garrison at Colchester. You're safe this far away, however! Soon after the grazing is replaced by arable land, a creek forces a left turn.

Just after the path goes through a little copse, you will come to a sign warning of a sea-wall breach. Do not rejoin the sea-wall! Instead, follow the permissive path to a footbridge that brings you to a road; turn right on the road, and left at the road junction.

The beach at Cudmore Grove

Ahead of you is the tidal causeway of **The Strood**. It often floods at high tide, twice a day, keeping the mainland at bay for up to an hour at a time. Built at the end of the seventh century, this was a

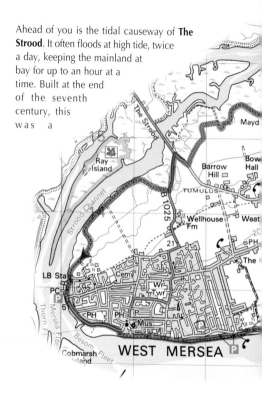

significant work of engineering for Anglo-Saxon England. Between 3000 and 5000 oak piles, each around 2m long, were driven deep into the clay, and compacted sand and grit laid on top to form a passageway. It is thought that construction was ordered by the saint-king Sæbbi to ease access to the minster at West Mersea. Successive surfaces have been laid on top since as the sea-level has risen.

About 450 metres from the road junction a path heads back to the sea wall on the right, at a concrete sign. Follow this to **West Mersea**. Turn a corner by a little black

weatherboarded cottage at Waterside and you come to the town's harbour area, busy with activity and with views across Old Hall Marshes (Walk 3) to Tollesbury. It's difficult to resist the temptation to break, either at one of the two waterfront pubs, or in a café, or, depending on the state of the queues to get in, the famous Company Shed, where fish and shellfish straight from the boats give the freshest taste of the sea imaginable.

Continue ahead on Coast Road, past another good oyster bar and a collection of houseboats. After the last of these, where the road climbs a little, take the path past the lower of two benches. This passes St Peter's Well, until last century the sole, and infallible, source of drinking water for the island. Turn up the steps after the well to visit the island's **museum**. Beyond the steps, follow the sign to Monkey Beach, heading along the shore past

35

*Beach huts,
West Mersea*

houses and, later, beach huts. The last of these are particularly attractive, with verandas, decorative wood turning, and a range of soft pastel shades.

When the beach huts end, go up to the sea wall and take the path through bushes and a greensward, rejoining the sea wall thereafter. This leads past a caravan site, towards a section which has been impassable since storms breached the sea wall in 2013. Instead, turn left at a waymark just under 300 metres from the caravan site, with a wire fence and Mersea Youth Camp (where up to 500 children might be staying under canvas) on your right. Follow this past right and left turns. Where the fence ends, turn right, and at a gate veer left joining a minor road which takes you past the Mersea Island vineyard and its café. Soon the road turns right then left at a farm; instead of going left, keep straight ahead at a concrete sign, which becomes a track through fields, with panoramic views over the island's coast. Later, keep a hedge on your right, and at a road, turn right and enter Coopers Beach Holiday Park.

In the park, ignore turns and join a hedged lane, which comes out to the park's café. Walk in front of it to join the sea wall, but when the park ends, continue with the right-of-way on the foreshore, eventually below low cliffs. Go up a slipway and you will be back at the East Mersea Flats board where you had joined the coast. Turn inland back to the start.

OYSTERS

Oysters were once so plentiful around the coasts of Essex and Kent that in Dickens' day they were a staple food of London's poor. Over-harvesting, disease and perhaps their reputation as an aphrodisiac – not just a matter of the shape of the flesh; they contain zinc, which stimulates testosterone – mean that production is now smaller-scale, and with it a reputation as a luxury food.

Within Essex, oysters are harvested principally in the Colne, Blackwater and Roach estuaries. The indigenous variety *Ostrea edulis*, held to be the most delicate in flavour, is known locally as 'Colchester native', although the species spreads from Norway to Morocco. They are only available to eat outside their summer spawning season, hence the adage that oysters can only be eaten if the month has an 'r' in it.

That does not hold for the other species growing here, the larger, less subtle, but perhaps more profitable Pacific (or 'rock') oyster *Crassostrea gigas*. Its habitat is between the tide marks, while natives are subtidal. Even so, they are now spreading, and breeding, beyond the farmed areas, and becoming a threat to the natives.

WALK 3
The marshes around Tollesbury

Start/Finish	Tollesbury, on Church Street (TL 956 104)
Distance	17½ miles (29km) or 7 miles (11km)
Walking time	7½hr; 3hr for the shorter route
Maps	OS Explorer 176/184, Landranger 168
Refreshments	King's Head and Lighthouse café in Tollesbury; bistro and two cafés at the marina
Public transport	Buses from Colchester, Maldon and Witham (not Sundays)

Tollesbury Wick and Old Hall Marshes, circumnavigated by this walk, are the epitome of Essex coastal marshland. Sea, bird and plant life all flourish here; as the day rolls on, the long level seascapes constantly vary, both from direction as the walk winds around little inlets, and from water-coverage as tides come and go; and with almost no 'turn-left-at-the-stile' navigation to worry about, your whole attention can be devoted to the air, the salt, the season and the senses.

From the **King's Head**, walk past the church, curving left so that you take the lane with the recreation ground on your right. This soon passes through **Bohun's Hall Farm**, where the 'private' signs do not relate to foot traffic. Just over 1km beyond the farm, nearing the sea, the lane splits: take the left-hand fork. Soon, take the few strides up to the grass-topped sea wall. Keep the sea on your right for the next five miles.

You are at the mouth of the River Blackwater, with the Dengie Peninsula directly ahead. Maldon lies six miles upstream, out of sight beyond Osea Island. The sea wall here probably dates to the Middle Ages, and was certainly extant in the 18th century. It's hard to ignore Bradwell Power Station, but even harder to imagine the coastline without it. Without pretending to be great architecture, there is a sculptural symmetry to its two buildings that becomes almost hypnotic as angles vary.

But there is so much more to concentrate on – changing light, little patches of cockle bank, the cries of duck and gull – that the natural world soon takes over. You enter the nature reserve of **Tollesbury Wick Marshes** just after turning back seaward from the inlet of Mill Creek. Just over 500 metres beyond, at a pill-box, are the remains of Tollesbury Pier, which once stretched 600 metres beyond the mud-flats until it was blown up as a counter-invasion measure in 1940.

Grazing cattle on Mill Farm Marshes

The **light railway** from Kelvedon arrived at the pier in 1907, hoping to attract pleasure steamers and packet boats, but trade never flourished. The line was cut back to Tollesbury in 1921, and even this struggled for business, finally closing in 1951, except for occasional freight to the Tiptree jam factory, which continued until 1962.

Just before **Shinglehead Point** (which, outside the April to August breeding season of the Little Tern, can be reached by a diversion from the main path at TL 987 103), the coast turns back towards Tollesbury. Old Hall

39

Marshes lie across the channel of Tollesbury Fleet. The boats huddled in Tollesbury Marina come ever closer; when you arrive there, follow the footpath signs past the Harbour View Bistro and then take the embankment by the road (high tides sometimes cover the road) past the

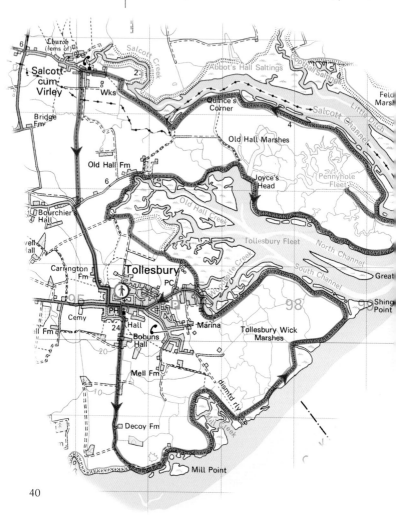

preserved sail-lofts. There is a café in the last of these, and another just along the road, although in winter the opening hours of both are more limited.

Shorter route
To complete the shorter walk, return along the road for about half a mile to the village centre.

Take the path heading away from the road at Tollesbury Sailing Club. The task now is to keep the sea on your right, not for five miles, but for eight. However, 'sea', or even 'estuary', may not always seem an appropriate term for the first couple of miles, as the tangled saltmarsh keeps only the most persistent channels from making landfall. Don't attempt to follow a couple of dykes seaward; they are remnants of an earlier sea wall, deliberately breached (as has happened elsewhere in Essex) to provide better flood protection, so lead now to dead ends. In these eight miles, the sole habitation passed is at **Old Hall Farm** and its adjacent red brick cottages. The marshes named from it are soon entered.

Old Hall Marshes have been in RSPB ownership since 1984. There are seven principal habitats, helping to secure a wide diversity of bird (and indeed plant and invertebrate) life: grassland, both improved and unimproved; reed-bed; coastal lagoon; saltings; mud flat; and open water. It's hard to overstate the role of the marshes for bird-life. In winter, internationally important populations of dark-bellied brent geese and ringed plover rest here. It's important too for many wildfowl and waders, such as goldeneye and curlew, and marsh and hen harriers are safe from persecution here. The marshes stood in for north Kent in the 2012 BBC adaptation of *Great Expectations*.

Tollesbury Marina

As with Tollesbury Wick Marshes, outlooks change with almost every stride. Looking seaward, Tollesbury Marina, West Mersea and Bradwell compete for attention; St Peter's Chapel can be seen too. Across the Fleet to the two Cob islands – part of the reserve – sapling stakes mark the location of oyster beds. After the tip of the marshes is passed, the only point where shingle and hence the open sea are apparent, the focus turns inland. The little hills on which Peldon and Great Wigborough sit are remarkably prominent, and the Tudor gatehouse of Layer Marney is in view as well.

Although it comes towards the end of a long day, take a 500 metres (each way) diversion towards the heart of the marshes. After the turn back inland, drop off the sea wall at steps, so as not to disturb waterfowl. Beyond a stile soon after (TL 991 116), a permissive path beckons you through a gate 'to viewpoints'. These are two hides, the second looking out towards the 50-acre reed-bed beyond **Pennyhole Fleet**. Both give the opportunity for a few still moments observing the comings and goings of the many species, and listening to the songs of those that cannot be seen.

Resuming the walk, slant back up onto the sea wall. Very slowly, Salcott Channel narrows. To reach the hamlet of **Salcott-cum-Virley**, turn off the sea wall beside overgrown steps, cross a footbridge and then go through a field on a grass strip. The churchyard here is a good opportunity for a final break.

Homewards is something of a repeat of the start, an almost dead-straight line, starting opposite the Old School House. Cross a field to the nearer telegraph pole and the stile beyond, then go through a gap in the right hand corner of the next field. Keep a reservoir on your left, cross a footbridge, then after a concrete track keep a hedge on your left in the first field and your right through two more. The path comes out to a minor road; turn right, then soon left at a junction. Stay on this quiet road back to Tollesbury.

BUZZARD, MARSH HARRIER, PEREGRINE

From the hide at Pennyhole Fleet, you're likely to see a buzzard or marsh harrier, perhaps even a peregrine, circle lazily in the sky, looking for prey. Forty years ago you would have been pressed to see any such thing. Even the most common of the three, the buzzard, was listed in the Essex Bird Report of 1992 as 'a scarce visitor at all seasons'. As the top predators in the avian food chain, they had been sorely depleted by insidious poisoning from agricultural pesticides leaching into their bodies in ever-greater concentrations from the small amounts in almost everything they ate. Persecution by humans, too, diminished their numbers. There have been significant revivals following bans on the most noxious chemicals and the introduction of criminal penalties for the use of poisoned bait or shooting.

The buzzard is now widespread across the county, principally as a winter visitor but with some now resident: research for this book treated the author to a spectacular late-summer display on Orsett Fen (Walk 7). Marsh harriers by contrast are more likely to be seen in the summer, as their name suggests on the county's coastal margins such as around Tollesbury, over-wintering in Africa.

Perhaps most enthralling of all is the peregrine, the world's fastest bird, reaching 200mph as it dives on an unsuspecting gull or pigeon, killing with a single strike of its hind toe deep into the breast. Like buzzards, peregrines are winter visitors: perhaps one or two pairs breed in the county. Like marsh harriers, they are principally birds of the coastal margins, although now starting to be seen inland.

The peregrine inspired one of the great nature classics of English literature, simply called *The Peregrine*, by Essex writer JA Baker. Written in the 1960s, Baker describes in prose of great beauty ten years of exploration of the Chelmer Valley, to search out the peregrine, determine its favoured places, and recognise its hunting patterns. He explicitly expected its local extinction. Alas, Baker died in 1987, before the current revival began.

WALK 4
St Peter's Chapel and Bradwell Marshes

Start/Finish	Recreation ground car park at Bradwell-on-Sea, by the village sign at the village entrance (TM 003 067)
Distance	10½ miles (17km) or 6½ miles (10km)
Walking time	5hr; 3hr for the shorter route
Maps	OS Explorer 176, Landranger 168
Refreshments	King's Head in Bradwell-on-Sea and Green Man at Bradwell Waterside; The Cricketers is on the shorter alternative
Public transport	Buses from Maldon and Burnham-on-Crouch (not Sundays)

This walk takes the sea wall from the little yachting harbour of Bradwell Waterside past cockle banks and saltmarshes – and a former nuclear power station – to St Peter's Chapel, the oldest religious building in Britain. From here there's a choice of return routes, the longer crossing Bradwell Marshes on its way back to the inland village of Bradwell-on-Sea, where the author Michael Morpurgo grew up.

Turn left out of the car park. With the **King's Head** on your left, walk out of Bradwell-on-Sea down its little High Street. At a road junction just past **Down Hall**, take the footpath heading half-left at a concrete sign. This goes through two fields, turning slightly right at the tree line between them, and comes out in **Bradwell Waterside** at the Old Post Office. Continue ahead past the Green Man

towards the quay, turning right on footpath 15 just before
Burnham Quay Yacht Club.

The walk now follows the sea wall for just over
three miles to the chapel, past **Bradwell Nuclear Power
Station**. ▶ Approaching **Sales Point**, 11 grounded barges
help prevent erosion of the cockle bank – 100 metres of
saltmarsh have been lost here in the last two decades;
it's possible to walk out to the closest barge at low tide.
At the outbuildings of the present-day Othona religious
community, keep to the cinder path to the derelict look-
out; the chapel is on your right.

The **chapel of St Peter on the Wall** was built in 654
by Lindisfarne monk St Cedd, using the Kentish ragstone of an earlier Roman fort (Othona) on the site.
Cedd became an important figure at the Council of
Whitby, which adjudicated on the form of worship
in post-Roman Britain. It fell out of religious use
in the 18th century and was used as a grain store,
but was restored as a chapel in 1920 and is today a
regular site of summer pilgrimage.

The power station
was decommissioned
in 2002 but there is
an intention to build
another here.

St Peter's Chapel

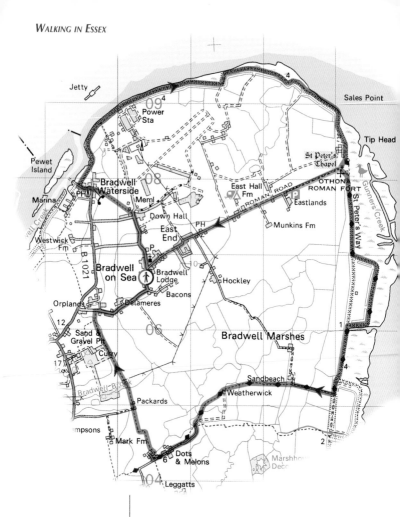

Shorter route

For the shorter route, take the track heading inland. This becomes a minor road at a car park, and continues direct (it is a Roman road) past The Cricketers pub back to Bradwell-on-Sea.

Continue along the sea wall: from the chapel, rejoin it by keeping the copse on your left. The copse shelters Bradwell bird observatory, which posts lists of recent sitings. Leave the sea wall at the Sandbeach outfall (TM 030 053), where a marker post points half-right down the slope, to a concrete track.

> From the Sandbeach outfall, there is a splendid walk, along probably the longest stretch of **uninhabited coastline** in southern Britain. It's nearly 12 miles without habitation or shelter to Burnham-on-Crouch – around 14 from the chapel. At times the saltmarshes stretch a kilometre from the sea wall, with low tide 2km further out. Sit for a while, and flocks of Brent geese may fly past you at head-height, and a barn owl come to explore at the peak of the day.

In 200 metres at a junction turn right towards **Sandbeach Farm**, but rather than make a further right turn to the farm, instead follow the St Peter's Way waymarks

Cockle spit, looking across to West Mersea

47

This walk passes both Bradwell nuclear power station and Bradwell wind farm – time for a healthy debate on the merits of each!

through two grass fields, with **Bradwell Brook** on your right. ◄

After that, keep to the left side of a field with a ditch on your left. Where the ditch ends, continue ahead to a barn. Head directly away from a breezeblock wall behind the barn to an earth bridge in about 200 metres. From here, head towards the large barns at **Dots & Melons**. The right-of-way makes a beeline for the barn but it's better to turn left on a track at the head of a hedgerow, and in 100 metres turn right at a junction, and follow the track to the barn. Here a minor road starts.

Some 250 metres along the road, just past 'The Cottage', turn right on a metalled track, following the waymarks right and left through Shingleford Farm, and continue with a hedge on your left. Cross a plank bridge and turn left onto a green lane for 80 metres, then right over a footbridge. Cross the field, walk past **Packards Farm**, continue ahead on a grass track, and go over a footbridge in a little glade made by Bradwell Brook. In the next field head towards the right edge of a wood. Enter the wood by a hurdle and continue along its right edge. Leave it by a footbridge and follow the path by three telegraph poles, veering slightly right at the last, to follow the right edge of the next field to a road. Turn right here back to Bradwell-on-Sea.

WALK 5
River Crouch

Start	Burnham-on-Crouch station (TQ 947 965): by bus or car, start at the clock tower (TQ 952 955), parking opposite or on Providence
Alt start/finish	Althorne station (TQ 905 979)
Finish	North Fambridge station (TQ 856 978)
Distance	10½ miles (17km) or 5½ miles (9km)
Walking time	4½hr or 2½hr
Maps	OS Explorer 176, Landranger 168
Refreshments	Pubs, cafés and restaurants in Burnham-on-Crouch; Ferry Boat Inn at North Fambridge
Public transport	Trains to Burnham-on-Crouch, Althorne and North Fambridge. Buses to Burnham-on-Crouch (not Sundays) from Chelmsford and Maldon

All the Essex estuaries offer excellent walking opportunities and here is an example from (Thames apart) the longest. It starts from the relaxed yachting town of Burnham-on-Crouch, includes an unexpected ascent, and then tracks past Bridgemarsh Island, once busy with agriculture and industry, but now abandoned after repeated flooding. After an inland stretch through a nature reserve, the walk ends at North Fambridge, It's easy to split the walk about half-way, for Burnham, Althorne and North Fambridge are linked by train.

Turn right out of the station and walk down Station Road and the High Street. Just before the clock tower, turn right down Shore Road, and then go right along the quay. The quayside twists and turns a bit as you head out of town but the way is always clear.

Map continues on page 51

49

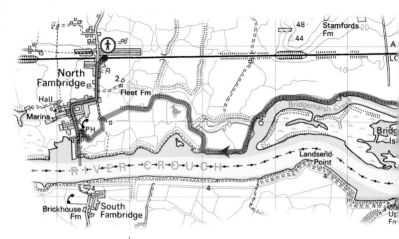

Burnham has four **yacht clubs**: you pass the Crouch and the Burnham-on-Sea on this walk, while the two 'Royal' clubs, Corinthian (a superb art deco building) and Burnham, have more favoured positions nearer the open sea. Over the river but linked by seasonal ferry from Burnham, Wallasea Island is the site of a new nature reserve created by the controlled breach of sea walls and the deposition of soil from the tunnels dug out for London's Elizabeth Line.

Beside Riverside Park, some fine houseboats are moored, and the Millennium Beacon is dedicated to 'the people of Burnham, past present and future'. Just past the park, the riverside path turns right to skirt the large basin of Burnham yacht harbour, dug out of the estuary in the late 1980s. Pass the large building that houses the Swallowtail bar before regaining the path, beyond the lifeboat station.

Back at the riverside, keep to the path until you come out to Ferry Road in **Creeksea**. In nearly 300 metres, at the drive to 'Tideways', go through a gate and continue on the left edge of a field until another gate leads you back to the river. Follow it to an unexpected rise, known

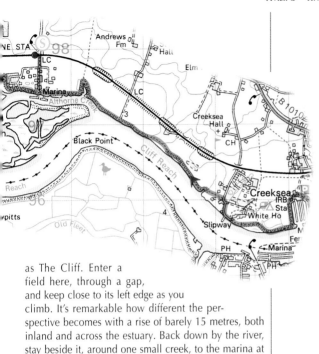

as The Cliff. Enter a
field here, through a gap,
and keep close to its left edge as you
climb. It's remarkable how different the per-
spective becomes with a rise of barely 15 metres, both
inland and across the estuary. Back down by the river,
stay beside it, around one small creek, to the marina at
Althorne.

Shorter route
Althorne station is just 400 metres along the lane from
the marina, if you want to start or finish the walk here.

Continue away from Althorne, skirting another small
creek. You're separated by another, larger creek – rather
than the Crouch – from **Bridgemarsh Island**, home to a
brickworks in the 19th-century; its chimney can still be
seen. Just before you return to the river proper, a sign
shows that you are entering Blue House Farm Nature
Reserve. About a mile further on, leave the sea wall at
wooden steps on the right (not the earlier, metal steps),
leading to a gate where a permissive path through the

North Fambridge Quay

There are three bird hides near the path, at least one of which should be visited for the intimate view of the waterfowl, waders and raptors of this marshland.

reserve starts. This is well waymarked, but there is one misleading waymark in the first field which points you left – the correct route is to stay on the right edge of this field and the next. Later, it follows a dyke-top path and crosses two fields to reach an information board by a car park. ◄

You can shortcut right here to the station at North Fambridge but that misses out its quay and pub, so instead take the path heading left. Go through the gate to the right of the farm and then continue ahead to the sea wall, reached up a flight of steps. Turn right to the quay, then continue on the dyke-top path above the road – which floods at most high tides – to the **Ferry Boat Inn**. Continue along Ferry Lane, take the second right onto The Avenue, and follow this left (as Fambridge Road) to the station.

WALK 6
Leigh-on-Sea and Hadleigh Castle

Start/Finish	Leigh-on-Sea station (TQ 831 857) or Two Tree Island car park (TQ 824 853)
Distance	8 miles (13km)
Walking time	4hr
Maps	OS Explorer 175, Landranger 178
Refreshments	The barge 'Gladys' at Benfleet; Hadleigh Park café and Hadleigh Farm tea room; Leigh-on-Sea High Street
Public transport	Trains from London Fenchurch Street and Southend-on-Sea, also local buses

There's something for everyone on this walk, including a downland park, Olympic site and medieval castle. It divides neatly into two halves, with the initial estuary section providing a panorama over the hilly second half. And unlike most walks, there's no need to stop at the finish – why not stroll down the seaside High Street, past cockle sheds to the pubs and galleries of Old Leigh, and, if it's summer, spend a bit of time with an ice cream on Leigh's little beach.

Leave the station by the exit to the right of the café and turn right. In 80 metres, cross the road and take the (initially) metalled track on the top of the dyke. In half a mile you meet a road that crosses a bridge to Two Tree Island. (If you have driven here, the car park is just the other side of the bridge.)

Once landfill, **Two Tree Island** is now part of Leigh national nature reserve, along with the intertidal Leigh Sands. Internationally significant for birdlife, it's important for reptiles too, including the adder. There is a thriving model aircraft flying club based in the west of the island, a rare example of co-existence for two very different forms of flight.

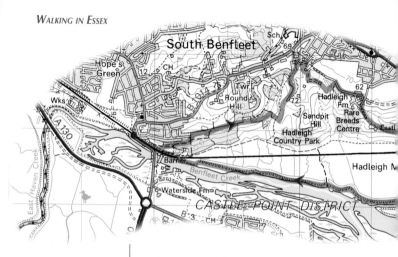

Continue straight ahead on what starts as a wide metalled lane but after 300 metres becomes one of the broadest dyke-top paths in Essex. At very low tide, you can walk through the western part of Two Tree Island and rejoin the sea wall by a ford at TQ 813 850 – but expect muddy boots. The way is clear until a gate marked 'Private' at Benfleet Moorings – the privacy does not relate to walkers, however. Continue ahead, on what is now Ferry Road, past the refreshment barge 'Gladys'. Some 40 metres beyond the flood barrier, cross the railway line from one metal stile to the other. The important Saxon victory of the Battle of Benfleet (894) probably took place in this area.

Alternative route
With a large or young party, it would be better to go through the subway at Benfleet station, turn right, then left up Station Road, and enter Hadleigh Park just before this becomes School Lane. Rejoin the walk at the line of benches mentioned below.

Over the railway line, take the thin path uphill through hawthorn bushes, into a meadow. Here turn right, but in a few metres fork half-left uphill to a line of benches and

join a gravel track. Fork left at the first junction and continue on the track for about a mile until you reach a green squeeze gate at the top of a little rise. Don't go through it, but instead go through the kissing gate to its left, onto a grass path. It contours high above a little valley reminiscent of downland (despite the lack of chalk anywhere close). Leave the valley at a cattle trough and enter woods, pretty with bluebells in spring, the path initially curving left. The car park for **Hadleigh Park** appears on your right; beyond it, go through a gate onto a lane.

You have been walking through **Benfleet Downs**, part of Hadleigh Park. The park's 500 acres combine

Testing event for the Olympic mountain biking at Hadleigh Farm

Hadleigh Castle

woodland, grassland, scrub, grazing marshland and saltmarsh. The diversity of habitats is echoed in the diversity of wildlife, including 27 species of butterfly.

The lane leads past a reconstructed Iron Age round-house, open occasional Sunday afternoons. Here turn right and go around the park's buildings (which include a café), keeping them on your left. ◀ At a T junction by a reservoir bank, turn right, then go left through the striped 'start' gates of the mountain bike course. Linger a while to see how the course uses the folds of the land to provide a test for all grades of biker. Take the second gravel path on the left, at a trim trail, and turn right when you reach farm land. Pass a row of white-painted houses and the entrance to Hadleigh Farm Training Centre.

The venue hosted mountain biking at the 2012 Olympics, and the course is now open to the public.

The **Salvation Army** established a colony here in 1891, where the poor of east London could learn agricultural trades and, because of the clay-rich soils, brick- and pottery-making. The colony closed in 1968; the present training centre was not established until 1990. A rare breeds centre is popular with children, and the tea room terrace enjoys views beyond the North Downs to the Greensand Hills in Kent.

Turn right down the road, dropping down to a squeeze gate. Continue on the track to **Hadleigh Castle**. At the castle, ignore the green gate left and instead enter the castle site by the gate in the metal fence 20 metres further on.

The ruins of **Hadleigh Castle** show how unwise it is to build large stone buildings on unstable clay. When the first phase of the castle was complete in 1232, it was a fine strategic site to protect the Thames from the French, with views from Thanet to London. Unoccupied by the mid-16th century, decay soon set in, but the present ruins make for an atmospheric site in any weather, and are the subject of one of John Constable's major works.

Descending to Leigh-on-Sea

Pass just to the left of the round tower, drop down left to go through double kissing gates, and head gently downhill on a broad grass path to a stand of oaks. Continue through two kissing gates in a hawthorn hedgerow and follow the left edge of two fields in the second; if the hawthorn is in bloom and there has not been too much rain, it's nice to slip for a while into an enclosed path just to your left. Eventually you come to a wide metalled lane, and finally join the road to the station.

Although now dwarfed by Southend, **Leigh-on-Sea** was far more important until the 19th century. As well as the delights mentioned in the introduction, it has literary claims as well: as the birthplace of John Fowles and where, on Marine Parade, HG Wells bought a home for his lover Rebecca West.

INLAND ESSEX

Willow plantation by the Colne (Walk 23)

WALK 7
Orsett Fen

Start/Finish	Orsett church (TQ 644 819)
Distance	5 miles (8km)
Walking time	2½hr
Maps	OS Explorer 175, Landranger 177
Refreshments	Whitmore Arms and Foxhound pubs, both in Orsett village
Public transport	Buses from Basildon, Brentwood, Grays and Purfleet

There was fenland in south Essex into the 1960s, and this walk visits the last to survive, Orsett Fen, and its near neighbours Bulphan and Stringcock fens. Even today, there is a sense of loneliness as you walk through this landscape, the low Essex ridges, although distant, seeming to cut you off from the wider world.

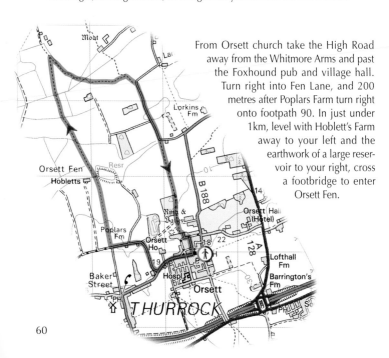

From Orsett church take the High Road away from the Whitmore Arms and past the Foxhound pub and village hall. Turn right into Fen Lane, and 200 metres after Poplars Farm turn right onto footpath 90. In just under 1km, level with Hoblett's Farm away to your left and the earthwork of a large reservoir to your right, cross a footbridge to enter Orsett Fen.

Orsett

The ditch that you cross feeds into the **Mardyke**, a Thames tributary about 1km to the west; it marks the fen's western boundary. Now reed-clogged, in Victorian times the Mardyke and the ditches running from it were navigable for the barges which supplied Hoblett's and other local farms.

Keep ahead to where the hedgerow turns right. Now cross the field half-left, heading for a point about 200 metres to the left of a copse, to find an earth bridge over a stream. Continue slightly left of the previous line to a footbridge, then (entering Bulphan Fen) cross two more fields on a similar line, in each case to footbridges. At the second of these, continue half-right until just before Judd's Farm, to a signpost. Turn sharp right onto footpath 89, with a ditch on the left. This becomes a track in the centre of a narrow field.

As you make your way across the fen, the **Langdon Hills** ahead begin to assert themselves. At 400ft, this is some of the highest ground in the county. The country park at the summit and the Dunton Plotlands nature reserve at the foot are both worth exploring.

The track leads to an earth bridge and, immediately beyond, a footbridge. Cross both and turn right into Stringcock Fen. In 60 metres, turn left, keeping a ditch on your left. At a junction signpost, go over a plank bridge and turn right on path 158. This brings you to Parker's Farm Road. Turn right here and continue along the road for about half a mile.

Approaching Judd's Farm

Where the road turns left, continue on signposted footpath 100, with a hedge on your left. At a gap in another half a mile join the track heading in the same direction, and later cross a farm track. Hereabouts, on private land to your right, is a Norman ring and bailey earthwork, said to be the site of a palace of the bishops of London. The reconstructed castle at Stansted Mountfichet is on the same pattern. You will soon come out to Malting Lane. Turn left for just under 200 metres and then take footpath 110 back to the church.

WALK 8
Havering-atte-Bower

Start/Finish	Bedford's Park visitor centre (TL 519 922)
Distance	4½ miles (7km)
Walking time	2hr
Maps	OS Explorer 175, Landranger 177
Refreshments	Café at the start; Orange Tree and Royal Oak in Havering-atte-Bower
Public transport	Buses 294 and 365 from Romford to Havering Park (TQ 500 922)

Towering redwoods, a herd of antlered deer, a Palladian mansion and some of the best views of a capital city to be enjoyed anywhere… and all just over two miles from the centre of Romford. The village of Havering-atte-Bower is surrounded by parks of different character, and two of them are visited here – the former royal parkland that is now Havering Country Park and the one-time private estate of Bedford's Park.

From the visitor centre, visit the edge of the deer enclosure and then take the path past waymarks 1 and 2, keeping the car park just on your right. Pass a yellow-arrow post into woodland and at post 12 turn right, keeping the park access road a few yards to your right. Continue towards the water tower ahead. Turn left when you

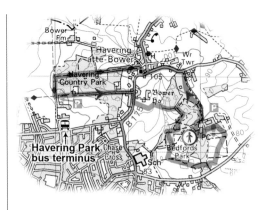

reach the road, enjoying the views over the Thames into Kent, until you meet the village green, stocks still intact, at Havering-atte-Bower.

There's no pretence in the '**atte-Bower**' of the village name, an ancient suffix denoting a royal palace. From the time of Edward the Confessor, Havering was effectively the eastern equal of Windsor. Successive royals to Charles I were attracted both for the quality of the hunting and the comforts of the palace, which stood to the north of the church. Indeed so popular was the area that Henry VIII ordered a second palace at nearby Pyrgo, which became more favoured; Havering palace was derelict at the turn of the 18th century, and Pyrgo lasted around a century longer.

Go down the lane between the riding stables and the church, picking up and following the London Loop signs for over 1km. The path takes you through a towering avenue of Wellingtonia redwoods, one of only two in England. ◄ Keep straight on until, soon after the redwoods end, so does the wood, with dramatic suddenness. In front of you is the valley of the Rom – unexpectedly rural for the location, with Hainault Forest beyond. To the left, picked out with clarity on the horizon, is every building of height

This mountain tree from the Californian Sierra Nevada, properly Sequoiadendron giganteum, was first brought over in 1853.

in the centre of London, spreading round to Canary Wharf and the Dome (O2). There is probably no finer spot to view the city, although there is a rival a little further on.

The redwoods of Havering Country Park

Turn left. Where the Loop turns right to cross the valley of the Rom (bridleway 277), turn left back into the wood. (If you have arrived at the Havering Park bus terminus, walk north on footpath 2, go past a metal gate, and turn right at the bridleway sign.) Just as the Wellingtonia avenue dropped downhill, this track rises, although through much more typical species. You come back out to the B175, this time at the Orange Tree pub. Cross and turn right here, and just past the entry to **Bower House**, turn left to re-enter **Bedford's Park** on an unsigned path. From the main road, you see the stable block of Bower House, and from a little way along the path, the Palladian mansion of 1729. They are both Grade I listed. Views immediately open up to the south.

In the dip, cross a little footbridge but not the second, and keep in the right-hand edge of the wood. At a wire fence turn, go through a kissing gate, and follow the path downhill to a plank bridge. Turn right at the next yellow-arrow waymarker, cross a footbridge, then turn left

Azure damselfly at Damselfly Pond

This is relatively new, dating to 1999, but is very popular for pond-dipping, and attracts dragonflies and grass snakes as well as damselflies.

where to go ahead would clearly mean entering private woodlands. Keep on the right edge of a meadow and in 40 metres take the first path right back into the wood. Pass post 4, and when you reach the open field at post 6, decide whether the views here are superior to those over the Rom Valley.

Turn half-left at the nearer gate, stay on the left edge of the next field to a metal kissing gate, and then keep a pond on your right. Cross a plank bridge and ignore right forks until you reach Damselfly pond, at post 8. ◄ From here, the yellow arrows lead you over a little stream to post 9. Don't turn right here but continue slightly uphill on a grass path through an unimproved wildflower meadow, richer in rare species such as pepper saxifrage and quaking grass than any other site in Essex. Go through two kissing gates, follow the path through woods, and after a walled garden – derelict for many years until its restoration in 2014 – turn left back to the visitor centre.

WALK 9

Hainault Forest and Lambourne

Start/Finish	Hainault Forest Country Park, outside the café (pay-and-display) (TQ 476 926)
Distance	6 miles (10km)
Walking time	3hr
Maps	OS Explorer 174, Landranger 177
Refreshments	Café at the start
Public transport	Buses from Hainault, Romford, Grange Hill and Chadwell Heath

Epping and Hatfield forests are the best-known remnants of the once-vast woodlands that covered much of the county, but another important patch survives, just the other side of the Roding Valley from Epping Forest. This is Hainault Forest, and like Epping it took concerted local action to save even the part that remains. This walk traverses the forest on its way to and from the delightful little church at Lambourne.

From the café walk to the pond, and half-circle it clockwise. Follow two signposts to Chigwell, turning left at the second. Go over a broad track in a cleared area and continue through the fence; at the next track, take the signed path towards to The Common car park. Look out for the tree sculptures: just before the path comes out into the open, Dick Turpin stands tall on your right. Essex-born Dick Turpin cut his criminal teeth in the county and references to him crop up on many of the walks in this book.

The Dick Turpin tree sculpture in Hainault Forest

Much of **Hainault Forest** was cut down after being declared as 'waste' by an 1851 Act of Parliament; within 50 years, nearly 5000 acres had been reduced to 800. A campaign to save what was left, led by an Epping Forest verderer, led to a 1903 Act that reversed the earlier provisions. Today, hornbeams, many pollarded, have pride of place, and there are oaks, ash and the rare wild service tree too; the forest is also one of the most important national sites for invertebrate diversity.

On the common, take the grass path heading right, cross a ditch, and take the left of two grass paths to the rarely used 'event car park'. Just beyond it leave the main path for a narrower path on your left, cross a footbridge and veer slightly right. Fork left at a path junction, go through a dip and come out at the Camelot car park at Lambourne End, opposite which is the Miller & Carter bar and steakhouse.

Take the minor road signposted Abridge. Beyond a dip, take the footpath heading right shown by a concrete sign, running on the left edge of two fields – a steepish little path from which you can see Hampstead Heath to the

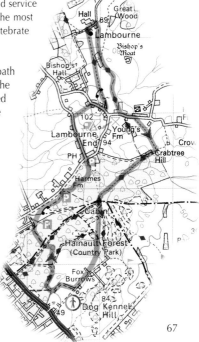

67

*Yellow flag iris,
Hainault Country
Park lake*

right of the city. When it comes out to another part of Lambourne End, turn right. Just beyond the houses turn sharp left and through a kissing gate keep on the right side of the meadow, looking across to Epping Forest, and the pretty white-plastered church of St Mary and All Saints soon appears. The path heads towards it, keeping a hedge on the right for the last 300 metres. Lam-bourne is one of those many Essex locations where church and the local manor house sit side by side some distance from any settlement.

The plasterwork on **St Mary and All Saints** dates from the 18th century, as does the present main door; the intention was for this quintessentially rural church to resemble one of the smaller London churches. The structure is of course far older, as the Norman arch to the former north door demonstrates, and the interior includes a 15th-century wall painting of St Christopher.

Turn right on the minor road, and right again where the road turns left. From Conduit Wood the bridleway becomes a green lane, running for well over half a mile to a road. Turn left here, and in 150 metres, just before you reach Tinoth Lodge, enter a field at a green gate. Keep to its left side for 80 metres and then cross to a hedge, keeping it on your left. As you descend the hill, enjoy the views over the Thames Valley, with the

The green lane south of Lambourne

69

North Downs beyond. The path runs through a gap and
between fences, then downhill (right) past houses.

At a signpost take the direction 'The Lake and Café'.
Keep right past a bench and in 150 metres, at a crossroads, turn left. At the next signpost, go through the fence
and continue down a wide forest ride, ignoring the first
path veering right but taking the second, through a tree-
belt, and coming out to an open area with a panoramic
view of Ilford, Canary Wharf and the City of London.
Now just make a beeline for the café, and see whether
you can spot the Orbit tower in the Olympic Park.

WALK 10

Mill Green and Writtle Forest

Start/Finish	Car park on Mill Green (TL 638 012), just north of the Cricketers pub, on the other side of the road
Distance	5½ miles (9km)
Walking time	2½hr
Maps	OS Explorer 183, Landranger 167
Refreshments	Cricketers and Viper pubs on Mill Green
Public transport	The Chelmsford to Ongar bus (not Sundays) stops at Metsons Lane

There has been little change in the landscape of and around Writtle Forest
– once an early medieval royal hunting forest – for hundreds of years. This
walk takes a loop through the woodlands, climbing out into Writtle Park,
where fallow deer abound, for a panoramic survey. The royal forest was
unusual in being surrounded by grazing plains, such as Mill Green Common,
where the walk starts and ends. Grazing ceased in the 1930s but careful
management is slowly re-establishing the lowland heath, an internationally
rare landscape type.

Walk away from the car park on the grass path and join Mapletree Lane, a wide but rough track; on this, you will pass a few houses on the left-hand side. At Maple Tree Farm, take the left fork, veering slightly right just beyond. The bridleway heads clearly through **Birch Spring Wood** to a road; cross over here and continue, through **Parsons Spring Wood**, on the concrete farm track. When you come to the wood edge, turn sharply right past a wooden hurdle onto a footpath which keeps just inside the wood back to the road. Cross the road – there is a bus stop here, if you are using public transport – and continue down Metsons Lane, past **Barrow Farm** and Metsons Cottage.

Birch Spring Wood

Turn left at the next road and then right along Cock Lane, taking the left fork at 'Elkins Cottage'. Keep ahead when you come to a smallholding (not left on a green lane), slightly uphill in the left edge of a wood, before coming into the open on the left edge of two large fields. At the end of a second, ignore the footbridge and instead turn right, soon coming to a farm road, where turn right again.

The farm road continues past a farm, with a former ice house in the field just after it; at the next house,

71

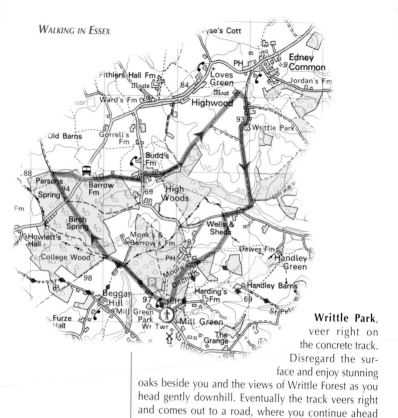

Writtle Park, veer right on the concrete track. Disregard the surface and enjoy stunning oaks beside you and the views of Writtle Forest as you head gently downhill. Eventually the track veers right and comes out to a road, where you continue ahead past Wells Farm. Take the first footpath left, over a plank bridge, shown by a wooden sign; it has a ditch on the right at first, before climbing to the edge of Box Wood. Cross a stile when you reach it, and keep the wood on your left over two more stiles before veering right onto a track after a modern house. Here you enter Mill Green Common; it is access land, so more interesting alternatives to the rights-of-way can be found.

Just 20 metres along the track, turn left onto a path at a wooden sign. ◄ At another wooden sign in another 20 metres, do not turn left as shown, but continue ahead on a path through holly. In more open ground it crosses the shallow depression of **Moore's Ditch**; 30

Keep on the track for 200 metres, round left and right bends, for the excellent Viper pub – the only one in Britain with this name.

metres beyond here, turn right at a path junction. ▶ The many pits in this area are the result of gravel and other extractions for brick- and pottery-making. After passing one of the deepest pits on your left, turn right on a more distinct path, and when this meets a gravel track, turn right for the car park.

Moore's Ditch is of uncertain age. Theories include a prehistoric boundary marker and a hindrance to Napoleonic invasion.

DEER IN ESSEX

These largest of British mammals are by no means uncommon in Essex, both in woods and on open land. Unless you stumble upon one – or more often a small herd – it's more likely you will spot them if you wait quietly, inconspicuously, at a time they are likely to be active (dawn or dusk).

Photo: Tony Morrison

Of the two native species, the roe deer is far more common than the larger red: there are a few of the latter in the Stour Valley area, and a breeding pair was known around Hanningfield, although the stag was recorded shot in 2012. It is not known why. There are red deer reserves at Layer Marney and in Bedford's Park. Fallow deer, between red and roe in size, were introduced to England by the Normans, for their meat and sport. Unusually, many of the Epping Forest population are black rather than buff-brown. The tiny Reeve's muntjac, which are about the size of a labrador dog, were introduced to Bedfordshire from China late in the 19th century and have since spread widely. They are sometimes known as 'barking deer', because of the noise they can make.

The antlers of the stags allow easy identification. Red deer have up to 16 points in a magnificent display, fallow deer antlers are flattened, whereas those of roe deer are short, barely a foot long, with usually just three points.

All deer, in Essex and elsewhere, are subject to culling; they now have no natural predators (except possibly the fox for a muntjac), and left unchecked can cause the widespread local loss of shoots and vegetation. Poaching and trophy-hunting keep deer numbers down too – both, these days, may have commercial imperatives.

WALK 11
Danbury

Start/Finish	Danbury Country Park (TL 771 047); by public transport, start at the Griffin Inn (TL 779 052)
Distance	10 miles (16km)
Walking time	4½hr
Maps	OS Explorer 183, Landranger 167
Refreshments	tea shop at Paper Mill lock; Griffin and Cricketers pubs in Danbury
Public transport	buses from Chelmsford, Maldon and South Woodham Ferrers

Essex has a hilltop village – and what a good one Danbury is. Who needs a jewel of the Renaissance deep in the Tuscan countryside when, 30 miles from London, you can tour sculpted estates, country parks and wooded dales, with views over what feels like all of Essex popping up now and then. As a bonus this route takes in a descent to the northern foot of the ridge, where the River Chelmer provides a delightful half-way interlude.

Facing away from the road, leave the car park of **Danbury Country Park** by the leftmost path, passing toilets on your right. Turn right, cross a stream, and continue ahead on grass. Through a kissing gate you pick up white-topped posts through the country park. Another run of white-topped posts comes in from left to right; when they do, follow the line heading right, coming out to the A414. The park was first laid out as a private estate as early as the 13th century. Much of it is now given over to Danbury Youth Camp, maintained by the County Council and filled with tents in the summer.

Cross the main road and walk down Riffhams Lane. Opposite Elm Green Lane, turn left at the concrete sign to cross **Riffhams Park**, landscaped in 1815 and one of the last works of Capability Brown's successor Humphry Repton. The path enters a wood at a stile and is clearly waymarked when it leaves, later turning left beside (not on) a minor road. Where you cross this road, take the 'Admiral McHardy Way' half-left across an orchard to the barn at **Great Graces**.

Here, cross the road and take the broad lime-tree path, **Grace's Walk**, heading gently downhill, aiming directly for Chelmsford. In just over a kilometre, this crosses Sandon Brook; 70 metres later, turn right at the wooden sign. ▸ The path crosses Waterhall Meadows to

The bridge over Sandon Brook is said to be haunted by Lady Alice Mildmay, who drowned herself hereabouts in 1615 to escape her husband's unkindness.

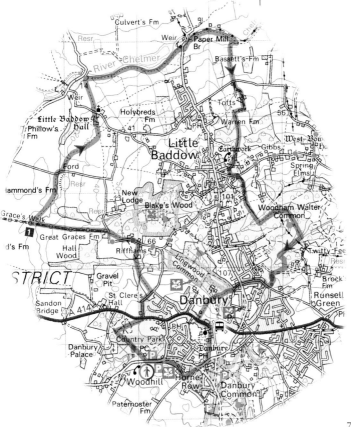

a **ford** on a minor road; there is a raised footway should the road be in flood.

> **Waterhall Meadows** are a rare Essex example of unimproved flood meadows. In summer, look out for the profusion of dragonflies and damselflies, particularly the white-legged damselfly. Eight species of warbler visit here, six to nest; at the other end of the scale, don't be surprised to see Highland cattle performing the essential task of keeping vegetation in check.

In the church, 20th-century plaster removal revealed fine timber roof beams and two medieval murals. In her memorial, Lady Mildmay holds a skull, denoting suicide.

Turn left at the concrete sign after the footway, crossing first a field half-right and then a paddock. Just before a modern house, turn left on a track and follow the waymarks through the fruit farm to **Little Baddow Hall** and church; as so often in Essex, hall and church are detached from the village proper, here a mile to the east. ◄ From the back of the churchyard, follow the path across a field to the River Chelmer.

Turn right on the towpath and follow it for nearly 1½ miles, passing the tea room and small marina at **Paper Mill Lock** just after half way. The river east from Chelmsford was

Little Baddow Hall

Hay stooks beside the Chelmer

turned into a canal in 1799; 12 locks account for the 75ft drop from the city to the sea. The stretch beyond the lock is particularly attractive, willows fringing the towpath and the slopes running up to Danbury drawing ever closer. Just before the river reaches leftwards, and 50 metres before a bench, turn right and keep a small wood on your right.

At a T-junction, the path turns left, with a ditch on the right, up to a minor road. Go straight over onto the bridleway, taking a couple of left forks to avoid houses, then beyond them turn right. Reaching a marker, turn left, and take a track, later fenced, at the right-hand edge of the common. From the top, just before you enter the woodland known as Heather Hills – little heather remains, but scrub is being cleared to encourage its return – there's an impressive wide view across much of northern Essex. Go ahead at a path crossroads and take the gravel drive of 'Old Rodney', taking a left fork to a minor road onto which turn left. Soon turn right onto Postman's Lane. Keep ahead in the first dip, and just beyond the second dip, having come in to Pheasanthouse Wood, turn left through a kissing gate.

You are now heading onto some of the most heavily wooded areas of the Danbury Ridge, and will encounter the black arrows of its nature trail, but not always in the order they are numbered. At the next kissing gate, entering the access land of **Woodham Walter Common**, keep ahead; 70 metres further on, turn half-left, and at the next junction, turn right onto a bridleway. You come to a pair of footbridges. Do not cross them, but turn right with a stream on your left, a path soon developing, and continue over a crossing track to enter Poor's Piece. Note the many horsetails hereabouts. From a boardwalk, continue ahead past post 13 and turn right at the top. About 60 metres further on – and 25 metres before post 14 – there is an indistinct right turn onto a path which soon improves. Cross the head of a sunken lane, turn left, and veer right to post 1. The path leads to a big sign about Danbury Ridge. At the road beyond, turn right.

At a junction enter **Lingwood Common** on a bridleway. Turn left in 120 metres, and after a fence ends, cross over a concrete track. Turn left when you reach the main road, and opposite the **Griffin Inn** go up the lane to

THE DANBURY RIDGE

From Danbury church, the gravel ridge runs east a little and then north to Little Baddow, maintaining a height of at least 300ft. There is development beside the ridge road, but away from that, the Essex Wildlife Trust and National Trust manage or own large tracts of commons and woods. Most are rated as sites of special scientific interest and many have open access. Lily of the valley flourishes across the ridge, and although under pressure, there are still good numbers of dormice here.

No two parcels are the same: Pheasanthouse Wood has raised bog of sedge and sphagnum moss, while next door the sessile oak woodland of Woodham Walter Common has developed over centuries by natural encroachment of trees onto the former open common. Here, as on Heather Hills, the return of heather is being encouraged. Pollarding in Poor's Piece may indicate that this area was once used as woodland pasture, as certainly was Lingwood Common – but in the latter, scrub and trees were cut for fuel, creating a slightly more open landscape.

the church. The church occupies the footprint of the Iron Age Danbury Camp, its earthworks alas almost lost, but what is not lost is the view southwards as you leave the churchyard by the footpath on its left, at the water tower; the high ground around Billericay – a continuation of the Danbury Ridge, geologically – is prominent, and sweeping westwards, the North Downs of Kent.

Drop down across the common passing the Cricketers Arms. Take the path shown by a wooden sign a few metres down Sporhams Lane. Cross a footbridge and turn right on a lane past houses. After the last house, take the path at the left edge of woodland, with good views southwards. Soon you come out to a road near the 'no entry' road sign for Danbury Country Park, where you finish the walk.

WALK 12

Moreton and the Matchings

Start/Finish	Moreton, near the Nag's Head (TL 533 070)
Distance	10½ miles (17km)
Walking time	4½hr
Maps	OS Explorer 183, Landranger 167
Refreshments	White Hart and Nag's Head pubs in Moreton; Fox in Matching Tye; Chequers in Matching Green
Public transport	No regular bus service; nearest stop is at Bobbingworth Mill on the Epping–Ongar route, 1½ miles south west

The three contrasted Matchings are a worthy target; the only question is where to start. Making use of a narrow north-south strip of a rare flinty gravel – less easy to cultivate than the boulder clay on either side, and left for a long time as common land – this walk starts from Moreton, once a Roman crossing-point over Cripsey Brook on the road from Sudbury to London. On the way out and on the return leg, you visit two churches now remote from substantial settlement in Magdalen Laver and High Laver.

With the Nag's Head in Moreton on your right, take the Harlow road, and then the lane shown by a wooden sign beside Gould Close. Keep on the left side of a field to a footbridge

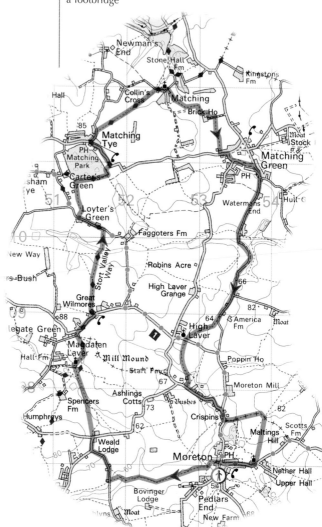

over Cripsey Brook and turn right, keeping the brook close by for more than a kilometre. The large house with an impressive brick chimney about half way along the brook path is **Bovinger Lodge**, which dates from the Commonwealth era after the Civil War. Eventually, turn right at a marker, and cross two footbridges, the second very substantial. Soon turn left onto a green lane to a minor road, where you then turn right.

Keep uphill on the road, veering right at a junction, until you come to the black weatherboarded barns at **Weald Lodge**. Here, just a few yards along the road heading left, a path leaves it on the right, at the right edge of a field – but there is no sign (TL 515 073). In a few yards you see a tennis court on your right. Go past an isolated tree in the field and continue down to a white post in the field corner. Go through a gap here, and continue to the **church of St Mary Magdalen** at **Magdalen Laver**. ▶

William Webb Ellis, creator of rugby football, was rector here from 1855 to 1870.

Leave the church by the kissing gate at the back of the churchyard, turning half-right across a field. Cross an earth bridge to, and follow, a Stort Valley Way waymarker. Turn left then right onto a minor road at **Tilegate Green**. Bear right at a junction, and at **Great Wilmores Farm** turn left at a wooden sign. The path soon keeps to the right side of two fields before crossing two footbridges and taking a clear cross-field path to a yellow post at a minor road, on which turn left. Leave this in about a quarter of a mile opposite 'Laughters', turning right on a clear path across two fields to the wood of **Matching Park**. Turn right, keeping the wood on your left; just after the wood turns left, keep on the left side of the field to come out to a minor road, following it left into the village of **Matching Tye**.

At the **Fox** pub, take the Sheering road, and opposite 'Hillcrest' turn right at a Forest Way post. This path runs without any excitement on a beeline for the hamlet of **Matching** – until, that is, you turn right to enter the hamlet itself. Suddenly, across a pond there is a near-perfect combination of church and the medieval marriage feast house, spreading oak in front, without a tarmac road to spoil it.

The **marriage feast house** is one of only four in England. It had lost its function by the late 18th century, but happily was restored in 1897, and now hosts other village functions as well as wedding breakfasts.

Turn right at a kissing gate (no sign) opposite the church sign, and keep on the right side of the field. Over a stile, a clear clear cross-field path leads to a tree-belt, where you should turn left between fields, coming out to a lane just to the left of a brick house. Turn left on the lane, then right on a path at a marker, and enter **Matching Green** on a fenced path between houses.

Saunter across the green, pass (or enter) the Chequers, take the lane past the school, and continue on the minor road signed as 'unsuitable for motor vehicles'. You're on this road for over a mile. Cars rarely venture down but, in exchange, you may have to paddle through the ford in wet times. Leave the road 120 metres beyond **America Farm**, taking the headland of a field shown by a wooden sign. Cross a footbridge, and go up steps. On reaching a pond, beyond which the hall and church at **High Laver** form a pretty view in winter; to reach them, keep the pond on your left and cross a field half-right at a marker. ◀

The philosopher John Locke lived his last years in High Laver and is buried in the churchyard.

82

MATCHING GREEN

The 14-acre green has been left largely unimproved, apart from the cricket pitch, and since the turn of the century improved management has seen species such as the common spotted orchid return. A survey of 2006 showed 25 species of grass and 87 of herb.

The houses around the green never crowd in on it and, with 28 listed buildings and many other fine houses, form almost a primer of vernacular domestic architecture over 600 years. Next door to the Chequers is the Elms, home to the artist Augustus John early in his career – and his wife Ida and their three young children, ten cats and sundry other animals, and from time to time John's mistress and model, Dorelia McNeill.

John Locke memorials at High Laver church

The path continues over a stile directly opposite the one you arrived by. Keep on the left side of a field, then, through a gap, veer half-left across a field towards its left-hand corner. Cross a stile, and then another by the larger of two gates, turning left onto a road. You can save half a mile by staying on this back to Moreton, but it's better to turn left onto a green lane just past Brook House. In just under half a mile at the top of the rise, turn right at the second gap onto a cross-field track to **Moreton church**, enjoying the southwards panorama as you amble back downhill. At the church, turn right past its splendid old rectory back to the village.

WALK 13

The River Stort at Harlow

Start	Roydon station (TL 405 105); or park near the village green (TL 408 102)
Finish	Harlow Mill station (TL 471 123); regular trains back to Roydon
Distance	5½ miles (9km) or 7½ miles (12km)
Walking time	2½hr; 3½hr for the longer route
Maps	OS Explorer 174, Landranger 167
Refreshments	Three pubs in Roydon, others at Burnt Mill Lock and Harlow Mill; tea rooms at Roydon Lock and the Gibberd Garden
Public transport	Rail services from Liverpool Street, Bishop's Stortford and Cambridge

The River Stort remains tranquil in spite of, or perhaps because of, a new town close by. Its planners gave good thought to natural boundaries and green corridors, respected to this day. This walk also gives a useful introduction to the sculpture heritage of Harlow, and a variation finish will take you to the remarkable Gibberd Garden, created by the first of those planners.

From the station at Roydon, cross the River Stort and walk up to the church and village green. With fine Georgian

Roydon village green

houses on the High Street, and the 15th-century weath-erboarded Church House in front of St Peter's, Roydon retains much of its character despite the inevitable infill-ing of a rail-connected village so close to the capital. The pubs are just a little further along the road, but to continue the walk, go down the surfaced lane behind the green. In 200 metres turn left and cross the railway. You come back to the Stort at Roydon Lock; cross, and turn right onto the towpath.

Map continues on page 86

The next mile is in Hertfordshire, and very attractive it is, through the nature reserve of Hunsdon Mead. You return to Essex when the towpath switches sides at Hunsdon Lock. At Parndon Lock (where the towpath switches again, but by now the boundary is safely to the north), you meet the first two of the five sculp-tures of the River

2

Stort sculpture trail: the sandstone *Flowing Onwards* (see photo) by Angela Godfrey and the beautiful glass-and-metal bridge *Over the Weir* by Alan Freeman and Karen Murphy. The whole setting, with Parndon Mill behind, is most attractive.

> **Parndon Mill** was mentioned in the Domesday Book, since when a succession of mills have stood on the site, replacement often following that occupational hazard of milling, fire. The present building dates from 1900 and milled to 1960. Now the mill is home to a thriving community of artists, sculptors, architects and designers, with a commercial gallery open daily except Saturdays and Mondays (other than bank holidays).

Burnt Mill Lock has a three-piece sandstone sculpture, *Short Stort Thoughts*, by Graeme Mitcheson. Here again change sides over the Stort – you need to use the road bridge of Burnt Mill Lane to do so; Harlow Town station is a few yards on. You are soon in the ancient hay meadow of Maymeads Marsh, part of Harlow Town Park. Leave the meadow through birch trees and continue on the path.

From here the park, its northern boundary always the Stort, is hemmed in to the south by industrial estates: but, so dense is the tree and shrub cover, it's often difficult to notice their intrusion. Turn left over a side stream on a footbridge, and immediately fork right. ◀ The path keeps close to the river, but is not always beside it. After seeing the Harlow Mill pub down to your left, you come out to the busy Cambridge Road.

To view the fourth sculpture, *Mill* by Nicola Burrell, go ahead instead of forking right, cross the river, and turn left to Latton Lock.

Shorter route
If you are not going to the Gibberd Garden, turn right here up to **Harlow Mill station**.

Look for the final sculpture, *The Flowing River* by Anthony Lysycia, on the lock island, and then cross the road and rejoin the towpath, which from here is on the

south bank. Stay on the towpath for about a kilometre, to just before a footbridge over a side stream. Turn right on a grass path and go under a railway bridge. The **Gibberd Garden** is about 400 metres after the bridge on your left hand side. It is open afternoons on Wednesdays, Saturdays, Sundays and Bank Holiday Mondays from April to September.

In the Gibberd Garden

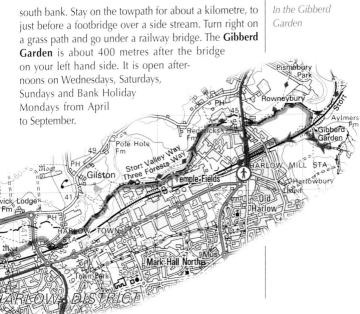

SCULPTURE IN HARLOW

Harlow is proud to call itself the world's first sculpture town, and this is no idle boast; no town in Britain has more public sculpture per resident. It is not simply a matter of quantity, for the relationship between sculpture, architecture and everyday living was integral to the vision of the new town's post-war master planner Sir Frederick Gibberd.

He and his wife Patricia established the Harlow Art Trust to build

'Flowing Onwards' by Angela Godfrey

up and maintain sculpture in the town, now comprising nearly a hundred pieces and growing. As well as commissions from contemporary sculptors – such as those seen on the River Stort sculpture trail – the collection includes works from figures such as Rodin, Elisabeth Frink and Barbara Hepworth.

Perhaps the best known work is Henry Moore's *Family Group* of 1954–55, unusual in that it is now exhibited indoors, in the civic centre; there is another Moore in the water gardens outside the centre, along with Frink's *Boar* and Rodin's *Eve*. There are many more sculptures in streets, shopping centres, schools and housing estates.

Although an architect of international repute – his other buildings include the Catholic cathedral in Liverpool – Gibberd made his home on the edge of the town he helped create. Ironically, he was refused planning permission to demolish the house, but instead redesigned it from top to bottom. In the surrounding gardens he and his wife created a series of outdoor 'rooms', in keeping with his overall vision of architecture; those rooms have contrasting styles and therefore plantings, using and alert to the slope of the site, each with sculpture pieces often commissioned for the setting by the Gibberds themselves.

To return to Harlow Mill station, retrace your steps to the railway bridge. Beyond it turn left, turn right through a kissing gate by the White Horse pub, and then go left. A few yards down the road, turn right on a fenced path to the station.

WALK 14
Hatfield Forest

Start/Finish	Layby on the B1256, just west of the Green Man, Takeley Street (TL 547 212); or use the National Trust car park (free for members only) at TL 546 202
Distance	6 miles (10km)
Walking time	3hr
Maps	OS Explorer 183/195, Landranger 167
Refreshments	Green Man pub; café by the lake in the Forest
Public transport	Buses from Stansted Airport, Bishop's Stortford and Saffron Walden (not Sundays)

Hatfield Forest is so good that it's worth delaying gratification a little. There are some pleasant waymarked shorter walks easily available from the National Trust, but this version starts outside, on a sweeping path with broad views of the forest, before traversing the full length of the forest and its varied habitats. After the Normans came, vast tracts of forest across England were commandeered for royal sport; but it is only Hatfield that retains, in large measure, the aspect that it had in the 13th century.

Opposite the Green Man, take the road signposted to Hatfield Forest, and cut up right to the old railway line just after the bridge. The site of the old Stane Street Halt is to your left, but you turn right, back across the bridge. The trackbed is now the Flitch Way, a bridleway (and linear nature reserve) from near Bishop's Stortford to Braintree. In half a mile, turn right at a marker and keep to the left side of two fields: Hatfield Forest is clearly visible over the valley of Pincey Brook. Beyond a fishing lake, look out for a marker post, where you cross a plank bridge, and then in 40 metres turn left and right at markers.

Over a stile, go half-left across a grass field and come out to the little common at **Bush End**, as tiny a

piece of access land as you will find. Follow the direction of the concrete sign to a footbridge in a gap and head across the field to an earth bridge. Keep ahead on the right-hand side of the next two fields and then turn right onto a concrete track to a minor road. Turn left on this, taking the right fork (for Woodside Green) when you come to a junction. Just past the house named 'Doodle Oak', enter Hatfield Forest by a gate. The house is named after a famous but now-deceased tree in the north of the forest.

As you will see, as befits a hunting ground, the forest is a mixture of denser woodland and open plains studded with shrub and the occasional tree. Initially, keep to a grass path across the plain which keeps a wire fence a few yards to its right, and in just after 300 metres continue on a path initially between fences.

In about 250 metres turn right onto the main forest ride. Very soon after you join a track, take a faint path left across the plain, **Forest Lodge** away to your left. Next take the ride heading slightly right between shallow ditches. Go ahead over the first ride crossroads, and turn right at the second. This leads you past the low mounds and ditches of the Iron Age camp known as **Portingbury Hills**, with much coppicing evident in the woods hereabouts.

> **Coppicing** helps secure a plentiful supply of timber without continual replanting. A mature trunk is felled near the ground; the tree's fully developed root system ensures that new shoots grow strongly; indeed, coppiced trees will live longer than uncoppiced. The practice also encourages wildlife diversity by enabling more light to reach the forest floor. Coppicing is especially important in Britain as indigenous varieties such as oak, hazel, ash, willow, field maple and sweet chestnut react well to it.

Turn right 100 metres after the yellow-ringed post numbered 11 (you will have seen number 12 at the Hills), soon forking half-left. Merge onto the lane coming in from the left, or better, stay on grass just to its right as far as you can. Soon a gate to your left leads to the café and

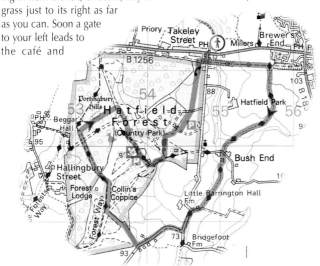

Coppicing in Hatfield Forest

adjoining Shell House, built in 1759 as a picnic spot for the Forest's then owners. Continue on the path by the lake; this becomes a boardwalk which ends at a lane. Don't join it, but continue on a grass path, crossing a lane. Just beyond the black-weatherboarded estate office (kept on your right), turn right onto the Flitch Way at a gate, pass Stane Street Halt, and return to Takeley Street.

WALK 15
Debden and Widdington

Start/Finish	Debden, village shop (TL 555 334) or Newport station (TL 522 335)
Distance	6 miles (9km) or 7½ miles (11km)
Walking time	2½hr or 3hr
Maps	OS Explorer 195, Landranger 154 and 167
Refreshments	Plough pub and Yuva restaurant in Debden; Fleur-de-Lys at Widdington
Public transport	Buses (not Sundays) from Stansted Airport, Saffron Walden and Great Dunmow. Trains from London, Bishop's Stortford and Cambridge

Debden means 'deep valley' in Anglo-Saxon, and it occurs twice in Essex; once in the Roding Valley, now a large housing estate with tube station, and here in the catchment of the upper Cam. As the name implies, some of the most undulating countryside in the county is to be found here. The neighbouring (and even prettier) village of Widdington hosts the remarkable Prior's Hall Barn, in use for around six hundred years until 1976, and now expertly restored by English Heritage.

From Debden's community shop, cross the road by the pond and go down the lane to the church. The route doesn't go through the churchyard (unless you choose to make a detour), but stays just above it. You come to an ornamental lake in Debden Park and turn left to cross it at a bridge. In 70 metres, turn right at a metal sign; the path soon rises up a broad grass strip towards a road on the skyline.

Turn right along the road, and just after a dip, turn left over a stile by a gate, passing the weatherboarded Midsummer House. Cross another stile (but not the one on your left a few yards on), continuing on the right edge of a meadow. ▶

The valley in which you are walking is that of Debden Water, a Cam tributary.

Trig Point above the Cam Valley

At a junction marker just over 400 metres beyond Midsummer House, don't go straight on but take the alternative half-left, which runs through the meadow until you meet a fence. From here, continue just a little higher up, on the boundary between arable and grass fields. At a path crossroads by a conifer plantation, turn left onto the green lane heading uphill to a road.

Turn left on the road and leave it at a large green barn on your right. The path goes ahead, at first with a hedge on your left, to a trig point. At 105m, this is not the highest point of the walk, but it is a good spot to see how the Cam Valley channels both road and rail routes, with the village of Newport nestling within it. Soon, through a gate you come to a lane; turn right onto it, and in 40 metres left on a grass bridleway.

Alternative start
Take the lane from the London-bound platform of Newport station past Briar Cottage. At the top of the hill, look for the trig point over to your left, and turn right onto the grass bridleway mentioned above (TL 532 331).

Take the footpath on the left at the end of the first field and turn right when you reach a minor road. In just under 200 metres, look for a concrete sign and former stile on your left. Walk across the field to a footbridge in the dip and then head towards the rightmost house. Here turn left and walk into **Widdington**. (If, at the former stile, the crops are impassable, stay on the road, veering left at the junction.)

At the village green, admire the harmony of this fine village before you leave. Tastes change; in the 19th century, there were protests that houses built on the west side of the main street spoiled the view. Then walk down Church Lane, fork left at the church, and turn right just over 100 metres from a telegraph pole, a ditch on your left initially. Continue across the field to a marker. Here, go through a gap in the field corner and keep ahead on the right side of a field to an earth bridge, after which you turn left towards the hamlet of **Rook End**.

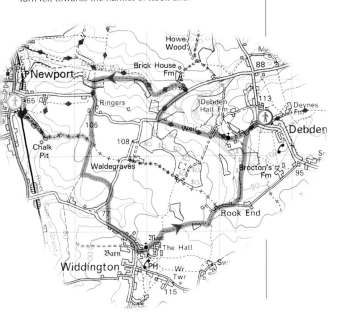

PRIOR'S HALL BARN

This barn, a magnificent testament to the craft of the medieval carpenter, is just off route before Widdington village centre. The barn is open on weekends between April and September and any opportunity to see the interior should be taken.

Mostly oak – four hundred trees would have had to be felled – not a single piece of ironwork was involved in its original construction. It's likely that it was built as a grain store for New College Oxford, which was endowed by the local landowner, the Bishop of Winchester, in 1379; New College only sold the site in 1920. The adjoining farmhouse is even older; its eastern wing was probably once a Saxon chapel, and it is thus a candidate for the oldest surviving house in Britain.

Other great Essex barns on or near walks in this book include Walton's barn in Ashdon (Walk 18), Cressing Temple barns near White Notley (Across Essex, Stage 6), and Grange Barn in Coggeshall (Across Essex, Stage 7).

Here, join a lane that comes in from the left. It soon becomes metalled and passes the impossibly cute Rook End Cottage; at the end of its hedge, turn half-left across a field to a footbridge. Cross it and turn left. The path soon becomes a delightful green lane heading through wood-land to an earth bridge. Turn right, and back on Debden's Church Lane, turn right again to the village.

Debden has a **lively community**. With nearby Wimbish, it's twinned with Tang Ting in Nepal; many Gurkhas are stationed at nearby Carver barracks (formerly RAF Debden), and this also helps to ensure the authenticity of the Indo-Nepali cuisine at the Yuva restaurant. The village shop celebrated its 30th anniversary in 2012 as the first community shop in Essex, and one of the first in the country.

WALK 16
Arkesden, Chrishall and Elmdon

Start/Finish	Arkesden, lay-by opposite the Axe and Compasses pub (TL 483 344)
Distance	11 miles (18km)
Walking time	5hr
Maps	OS Explorer 194, Landranger 154
Refreshments	Axe and Compasses at Arkesden; Red Cow at Chrishall
Public transport	None

From Arkesden, one of the prettiest villages in the county, this walk slowly climbs via an old corpse road to the highest point in Essex. Long sweeping views from here beckon you on to Chrishall, before a stretch of the Icknield Way Path – and a surprising glimpse of Cambridge down below to the north – takes you into Elmdon. The return takes you through paddocks and an avenue of horse chestnut trees.

With the **Axe and Compasses** pub to your left, walk out of the village, taking the minor road signposted to

Duddenhoe End. Some 200 metres past the drive to **Chardwell Farm**, turn left along a green lane.

This is Steven's Lane, a former **corpse road** on which the coffins of the departed were taken to burial in Arkesden church. Corpse roads are more familiar to walkers in the north of England – there are famous examples in the Lake District, and the Pennine Way relies on one near Alston.

Steven's Lane comes to a road-end at 'Little Fosters'. Turn left here, not on the private drive, but on a green lane that runs parallel. Ignore a footpath heading left, but when the green lane turns left, go right through a gap.

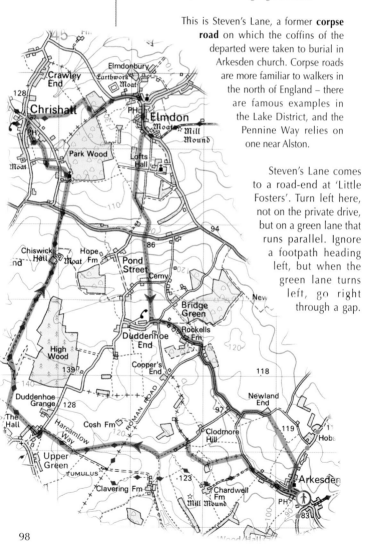

▶ Keep to the left edge of a field. You come to a broad track, a former Roman road; turn left on it for 25 metres, and then leave it half-right, to follow the right edge of a field.

Turn right when the path ends at a wide cart track, round a bend left to a gap. Here, as a little marker shows, move to the left side of the hedge. After a gate and later a kissing gate turn left on the road and enter Langley Upper Green. In 100 metres turn right on an unmade road past large houses. After 'Boundary House' turn right then almost immediately left. The path is then fenced before crossing fallow ground and then keeping to the right edge of a field. Turn right at the next path junction, and again keep to the right edge; you come to a broad belt of trees at the end of the field, and enter it at a wooden marker, to come out into another field. This is Chrishall Common, the roof of Essex at 482ft/147m!

Many enjoy the nationwide exercise of **climbing the county tops** of Great Britain – they include hills and mountains as well as varied lowland spots such as this. For more information see the Cicerone guide by Jonny Muir.

Here, you join the waymarked Harcamlow Way (see Appendix C), and follow it to Chrishall.

Arkesden

99

The path ahead soon becomes a good broad track with Chrishall church in view a mile away. The path skirts **Chiswick Hall** – keep the swimming pool on your right and the show-jumping area to your left – and keeps to the left side of a hedge before joining its drive. At the B1039 continue over a footbridge just to your left.

Enter **Holy Trinity Church** and you will immediately be surprised by what appears to be a Rubens original. It is alas a copy, by Ramsay Richard Reinagle (1775–1862), but a very fine one.

Leave the church not past the cottage but through a gap with a kissing gate. After another, cross the minor road, go ahead initially on a fenced path, and after a right turn cross another minor road. The path eventually goes through a gap on the right, passes a flint cottage – from the Common, you have been in chalk country – and continues down a lane to the thatched **Red Cow** pub in the centre of Chrishall.

Now you join the Icknield Way Path. From the war memorial, follow its waymarker down Loveday Close, and turn right after Marchpane House. Continue on the left edge of a field, across a stile and between fields. Cambridge can be seen to your left – surprisingly far below. Enter a wood and turn right, then left at the next junction, to come out to a road, and continue ahead into **Elmdon**.

Elmdon was named for its **three elms**, local folklore insisting there were no other elms in the county. This was never true, and although Dutch Elm disease led to devastation, there is a minor recovery in progress. The Dial pub is currently (2018) closed but there are plans to re-open it.

Turn right down the High Street, enter the cricket and football field opposite Wilkes Barn, and leave it at a kissing gate beside an oak. The path continues between paddocks to a stile and footbridge. Keep on along the

left edge of a field to come to a hedge surrounding Mill House; keep the hedge on your right, and cross the B1039 once more. Ahead the path continues inside an avenue of horse chestnut trees. When this ends keep to the right edge of a field, cross the minor road, and continue across the centre of two fields (no path) to another minor road at **Duddenhoe End**.

Inside the horse chestnut avenue

Turn left, and at the junction ahead go ahead along the gravel lane, which leads past Rockells Barn to **Rockells Farm**. Here, continue on the farm lane to a minor road, onto which you take the left fork. You can stay on this very quiet road for a mile and a half back to Arkesden, but it's much better to take the left-hand fork at a junction half way to the house of **Newland End**. Take the second footpath right, opposite the drive. This passes a solitary ash tree and keeps a dead-straight line across the field with good wide views over the start of the walk. At the road turn right and pass the delightful cluster of cottages by the church, finishing off with the village stream on your right so that you do not retrace your steps.

WALK 17
Great Chesterford and Saffron Walden

Start	Great Chesterford, near the church (TL 506 428), or at the station
Finish	Full route as above; shorter route Saffron Walden High Street (TL 537 383)
Distance	13 miles (21km) or 8½ miles (14km)
Walking time	5½hr; 4hr for the shorter route
Maps	OS Explorer 195/209, Landranger 154
Refreshments	Crown & Thistle in Great Chesterford; café at Audley End House; many options in Saffron Walden
Public transport	Train to Great Chesterford; buses link Saffron Walden and Great Chesterford

There are plenty of short walks anthologised around Saffron Walden and Audley End, but why not make a day out of it around the upper Cam valley? This route takes you from Great Chesterford – once an important Roman garrison, early in the occupation – along the Icknield Way Path to Strethall, before heading to the great house at Audley End. The old market town of Saffron Walden is now not far away, and from here the route heads uphill for the views, before a section beside the Cam takes you back to Great Chesterford.

In Great Chesterford with the **church** on your left, walk along Church Street, turn left into Newmarket Road, and take the road signposted to Ickleton. (If you come from the station, take the Ickleton road from the end of the station approach.) Cross the level crossing and immediately turn left, signposted for the Icknield Way.

Beyond Smock Mill House, this becomes a green lane, although soon it has to curve left to a bridge over the **M11** and then come back to resume the same line. As you leave the motorway behind, the contrast between it and this ancient trackway – undoubtedly Roman, if not the Iron Age Icknield Way itself – could scarcely be greater. If there is summer undergrowth in the green lane, use the headland on the right. The green lane ends at a marker a kilometre from the bridge and the path then heads half-right across a field to a minor road. Turn left on the road, go ahead at the crossroads, and soon turn right towards the Saxon church at **Strethall**.

> The antiquity of the **church** is celebrated in the dates of the altar cloth, 1010–2010; the tower's two bells were cast in the 1350s and still ring true. At six hundred acres, Strethall may well be the smallest parish in the country; it's certainly one of the few dozen 'thankful villages', which lost no residents in the carnage of the First World War, hence the lack of a war memorial.

Just before the church, turn left onto a sunken green lane, the church above to your right. At a concrete sign turn right across a field to where another green lane starts, turning left onto it. Where it meets a track, turn

Great Chesterford

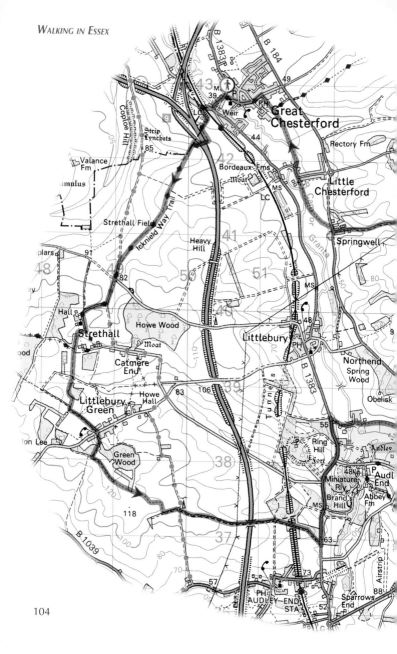

left, and then in 20 metres right, onto a lane between hedges. After a dip, you come to a coppiced wood on your left and a hedge on your right. Keep by the hedge as it moves away from the wood, and then veer left at a path junction. Go through a meadow and enter the hamlet of **Littlebury Green** through a coppice cathedral.

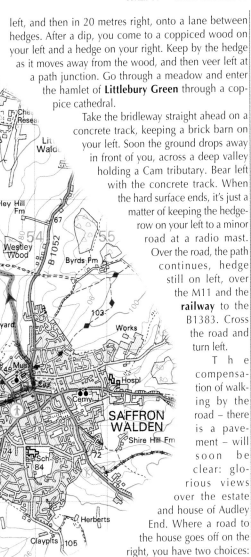

Take the bridleway straight ahead on a concrete track, keeping a brick barn on your left. Soon the ground drops away in front of you, across a deep valley holding a Cam tributary. Bear left with the concrete track. When the hard surface ends, it's just a matter of keeping the hedgerow on your left to a minor road at a radio mast. Over the road, the path continues, hedge still on left, over the M11 and the **railway** to the B1383. Cross the road and turn left.

The compensation of walking by the road – there is a pavement – will soon be clear: glorious views over the estate and house of Audley End. Where a road to the house goes off on the right, you have two choices:

AUDLEY END

When built in Jacobean times for the first Earl of Suffolk, this mansion was on the scale of a royal palace. Although gradually reduced in size during the 18th century, it is unquestionably one of England's grandest stately homes, following substantial remodelling of the gardens by Capability Brown, and of the interior by Robert Adam. Its owners, later the Lords Braybrooke (still resident on the estate, gifted to the nation in 1948), guarded the park so effectively that a London-to-Cambridge canal was never built and the main railway line was diverted away from Saffron Walden.

In war time the house was home to the Polish branch of the Special Operations Executive, and a memorial to their fallen can be found in the grounds.

continue on the B road; or turn right to visit the grounds and perhaps the house too. Entrance is free to English Heritage members and Art Pass holders.

Leave the road on the lane to Home Farm. Don't go into the farm, but at a marker keep ahead with a stream on your left. After the stream moves away in about half a mile, cross a footbridge and continue on a grass strip to a gatehouse. Here you enter **Saffron Walden** along Abbey Lane. Turn left onto the High Street.

Shorter route
If you are finishing here, upon reaching the High Street, go right instead of left for the bus stop for Great Chesterford.

Turn right onto King Street into the Market Square. Take Rose & Crown Walk (by Boots) out to The Common, and turn left. ▶ This leads you past the remains of the Norman **castle**; just beyond, turn left onto Catons Lane. Continue through the car park of the town football club and over a stream veer right onto the hawthorn-hedged path running north out of town. From time to time, look back for a retrospective of the town.

By a chalk quarry, turn left on the grass headland, then right at the metal sign towards **Springwell**. When the path levels out, and just before you reach a line of pylons, turn left on a wide track which keeps to the right

At the far side of The Common is the largest turf maze in Europe – but be warned, navigating it adds a mile to the walk.

Westley Wood

edge of a dry valley (not the track in the very bottom of the valley). Later a short stretch of green lane leads you out to the B184, where you should turn right for a few yards and left at a concrete sign.

This path climbs briefly before dropping down to the River Cam. Aim now to the right of the chapel in **Little Chesterford**, going through a kissing gate and along the road. Before this crosses the Cam, veer right at a wooden sign, and at a marker keep to the right edge of a field. This enters Great Chesterford at its High Street; turn left, past the **Crown & Thistle** and a host of other fine buildings, back to the church or station.

SAFFRON WALDEN

As the site of a small Anglo-Saxon town and with a strategic location in the undulating lands of the upper Cam valley, Saffron Walden was a natural choice for a Norman castle. Soon it took over the market charter of Newport a few miles upstream, and enlarged away from the castle environs out towards the abbey where Audley End House now stands – the 13th-century 'repel ditches', seen to the right of the Abbey Lane gatehouse, marked the new boundary.

Fairfax and Cromwell met here in 1647 and – influenced by the rank-and-file of the New Model Army – averted a split in the Parliamentary ranks over whether to march on London. A strongly non-conformist town from an early date, the Quaker Gibson family secured the building of the Town Hall and museum.

Earlier known by the market designator of Chipping Walden, the 'Saffron' of the present title refers to the rare and expensive spice extracted from the crocus, widely cultivated here in the 16th and 17th centuries. This, the earlier wool trade, and in Georgian times malt and brewing, were the mainsprings of the town's early wealth. This is seen today in the parish church, the largest in the county, and numerous fine buildings – although sadly the 15th-century, half-timbered, Grade I listed youth hostel closed in 2011 to become a private home.

WALK 18
Ashdon

Start/Finish	In the village centre, outside the Rose & Crown pub (TL 587 421)
Distance	6 miles (10km)
Walking time	3hr
Maps	OS Explorer 209, Landranger 154
Refreshments	Rose & Crown pub
Public transport	Buses from Haverhill, Saffron Walden and Audley End, not Sundays

Ashdon is a small and ancient village with many highlights. On this walk you will take in the medieval guildhall and hilltop windmill as well as the village centre, huddled into the valley of the little River Bourn. From the guildhall the walk takes two green lanes into the fine open country to the north of Ashdon, and another brings you back.

With the **Rose & Crown** on your right, walk down the main village street. At the village **museum** – once the Labour Hall, Ashdon being a key site in the agricultural strike of 1914 – turn left on a path. Do not cross the foot-bridge, but turn right into the field, veering rightish. At the top, go through not the large gap on the left but a smaller one next to it, on a fenced path to the church. The timber-framed 15th-century **Guildhall** is in front of you, a lovely setting. ▸

Walk through the churchyard to a road and turn right, then left onto Fallowden Lane. Past Fallowden Farm are the platform and waiting room of the former Ashdon Halt, closed since 1964 but still just about standing. Don't go down the railway line though; instead, continue on the bridleway past Halt Cottage a few yards to a path junction, where you need to turn left, then right down a gravel track; where it ends, turn a quarter-right onto the

The Guildhall had a relatively short life as a public building, being converted to tenements in the early 1700s, later the parish workhouse, and a private home since the 1950s.

The cairn above Bowsers End

first of the walk's green lanes. Turn right where the lane meets a farm road, and veer slightly right after the farm.

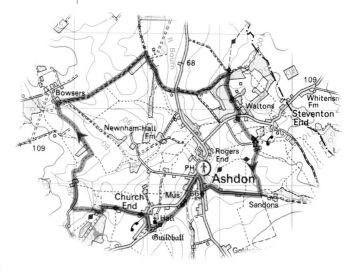

Keep to the left side of a field for nearly a hundred metres before crossing it half-right at a marker. Cross a plank bridge at another marker and enter the second green lane; when it ends after a little copse, keep to the right edge of two fields, finally crossing a third to the imposing **Great Bowsers farmhouse**. Here, turn right on a bridleway, initially concrete, later grass. It passes one of only two known cairns in the county, made out of redundant rubble! For setting, it might not provide summit-to-summit views, but the coun-tryside hereabouts is broad and open, especially to the north and east.

The bridleway passes a wood on the right. At the end of the wood, turn right to join the farm road coming out of the house (Lang Meadows) in front of you. When you come to a road, cross it and continue on the bridleway indicated by a wooden sign just to your left. In 300 metres take the left fork, so that you keep the wood on your right. In a further half a kilometre you come to a path junction: turn right here, onto a broad beech avenue past the grand house known as **Waltons**.

Ashdon Windmill

THE FARM WORKERS' STRIKE OF 1914

The stories of labour unrest – among matchgirls, dockers and miners – in industrial centres are deeply embedded in our social fabric. Less well-known are the rural struggles. This corner of Essex was at the heart of the national agricultural strikes of 1914.

At the start of the 20th century, farm wages in Essex were among the lowest in the country: 13 shillings a week, kept there by farmers' use of lock-outs and evictions. In late 1913, workers formed a branch of the National Agricultural & Rural Workers Union at Helions Bumpstead, and struck for a wage of 16 shillings a week. The strike soon spread across the villages of north Essex and into Cambridgeshire and Suffolk. Villages supported each other, with processions, union banners and red flags waving, torchlights glowing at night, and songs being sung. The likes of future Labour leader George Lansbury and suffrage leader Sylvia Pankhurst led rallies.

As the summer wore on, the farmers feared the harvest would rot in the ground. Some welcomed this for teaching the workers a lesson – 'Rather than pay/I'll waste all my hay', as one London paper caricatured this attitude. Others grew desperate. At Ashdon, the farmers tried to bring in hundreds of strike-breakers: 70 police officers were billeted at the Rose & Crown to protect them, and eight Ashdon men were fined at Saffron Walden court for picketing. Seven were sent to jail for non-payment, the other taking the commutation of Army service.

With war imminent, talks began in earnest at last, and the strike was settled a day before its declaration. The workers secured 15 shillings a week plus £8 for bringing in the harvest, but not all strikers were re-employed.

This smock mill dates from 1757 and was active to 1912; it has been in village ownership since 2000 and has since seen significant restoration.

Cross a minor road beside another of the great Essex barns, continuing over two stiles into a field, which cross to **Ashdon Windmill**. ◄ From the mill cottages, take bridleway 70 (wooden sign); this is the longest and muddiest of the walk's green lanes. Follow it into a dip, where turn right on a minor road, and right again at the next road junction to return to the village centre.

WALK 19
Radwinter and Bendysh Woods

Start/Finish	Recreation ground car park at Radwinter, entrance opposite the school (TL 606 373)
Distance	5½ miles (9km)
Walking time	2½hr
Maps	OS Explorer 195 and 210, Landranger 154
Refreshments	Plough Inn, Radwinter
Public transport	Bus from Haverhill and Saffron Walden (not Sundays)

A devastating fire of 1874 changed Radwinter forever. It provided the Arts & Crafts movement architect William Eden Nesfield with the opportunity to rebuild the village centre in accordance not only with its aesthetic principles but its social ideals too. All village services were grouped around the crossroads – although sadly only the community hall retains its original function. This walk links this remarkable village to the two Bendysh woods, home to red, roe, fallow and muntjac deer as well as the elusive oxlip and many species of orchid.

With the school beside you on your right, walk out of the village along Water Lane. This little road crosses over two fords, with footbridges for times of flood, and passes several pretty houses. Turn left when it joins a larger road just past a row of thatched white cottages, and ignore the turning to Radwinter End. Instead, turn right at a footbridge on a path shown by a wooden sign. Switch over to the left side of the ditch in 150 metres, soon keeping a small area of conifers to your right. Proceed to the corner of **Little Bendysh Wood**, and turn left along the edge of the wood to a pond.

Take the path heading right from the pond over a log bridge to an area of laid logs, and then continue along the right edge of the wood (no path) until a ride (not shown on the OS map), where you then turn left. When you

113

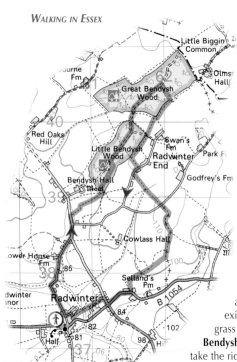

reach a crossroads of rides, turn right. (An easier option is to continue past the pond with the wood edge on your right until a gate, and turn right onto a ride here; however, the 100 metres before the gate, although on a wide headland, is not a right of way. When you reach the ride crossroads mentioned above, continue straight ahead.)

From the ride crossroads, continue through the wood (ignoring a crossing footpath, and a ride heading left, not shown on the OS map) for more than half a kilometre to a fork; take the left fork. You soon exit the wood, and continue on a grass path by a ditch to enter **Great Bendysh Wood**. At a fork in 40 metres take the ride on the right, through a wooden fence. At the next fence, in over 400 metres,

Little Bendysh Wood in autumn

114

Radwinter Church

turn right, and turn right again when you leave the wood, keeping to a path which has the wood on your right.

There is a path junction where the wood turns right in 250 metres. Head straight across the field to the left edge of Little Bendysh Wood, and keep this on your right for over 300 metres, turning left across the field where a footbridge enters the wood, aiming for the right-hand side of an evergreen garden hedge. Turn right onto the minor road at **Radwinter End**, then left on a path after Willow House, veering half right at the second gate and then crossing a footbridge. Make a straight line across

115

the field, over another footbridge, and at a road continue ahead onto a green lane.

Ignore the paths at a marker post but 250 metres beyond it (no sign), veer half right onto a grass strip, picking up a hedgerow on your right. Follow this to the end of the field, turn left, cross a footbridge and then turn right on the **B1054**. At the crossroads by the Plough Inn, turn right, taking a path left (no sign) just beyond Old Chapel House. Turn right at an outbuilding, then

OXLIPS

Essex is rightly famed for its bluebell woods, but that plant is hardly rare in England, if threatened by hybridisation. Oxlip woods however, of which the two Bendysh woods are prime examples, are restricted to the small patch where Essex, Suffolk and Cambridgeshire meet, and threatened even there – at least in part, due to the numbers of browsing deer. If you see an oxlip-like plant elsewhere in the county, it is either a cowslip or its hybrid with the primrose.

Look out for the light yellow flowers, a little like the primrose but in clusters on each stem, from late March to May. The plant was once so common in Great Bardfield (Walk 21) that it was known as the 'Bardfield oxlip'; a project is in hand to re-establish it there.

over a ditch go immediately left. Cross a footbridge, which brings you out to a new estate. Take the path by house 17, join a cul-de-sac, then turn left and left again back to the school; but don't leave without seeing the church porch, a complete surprise and another of Nesfield's works.

WALK 20

Thaxted and Great Easton

Start/Finish	Thaxted Guildhall (TL 611 309); parking on Margaret Street (TL 611 311)
Distance	9 miles (14km)
Walking time	4hr
Maps	Explorer 195, Landranger 167
Refreshments	Several pubs and cafés in Thaxted; Swan at Great Easton; Three Horseshoes at Duton Hill
Public transport	Buses from Saffron Walden, Bishop's Stortford, Stansted Airport and Great Dunmow (not Sundays)

The historic and still-thriving small town of Thaxted occupies a rib of ground above the infant River Chelmer, which rises three miles to the north-west. This walk heads out on the higher ground to the east of its valley, passing through farmland with wide views. The village of Great Easton, which like Thaxted nestles above the river, lies just over half way and it too has many fine buildings. On the return, the walk passes the site of the ancient abbey at Tilty before keeping to the riverbank almost all the way back.

With Thaxted Guildhall and the **parish church** behind you, walk along the main road out of town, following it round past the garage. Turn left on a track opposite Totman's Farm and then turn right at a line of poplar trees. Just over 100 metres after a crossing path, switch to the right-hand side of the hedgerow at a marker. In a dip, turn left over a footbridge and in another 100

Thaxted's Stoney Lane rises from the Guildhall to the church

metres turn right at a marker. Take the metalled path through **Richmond's Farm**, turning right onto the farm road.

Veer right at a junction and just past 'Greenways' turn left onto a footpath, keeping to the left side of a ditch. Turn right over an earth bridge and continue into and through **Sibley's Green Farm**. This becomes a minor road. Turn left on a metalled track at 'The Shieling'. When this turns left, continue ahead through the elm trees, straight across the field to a footpath marker in the hedgerow opposite (about 150 metres). Veer slightly right across the next field and, where it ends, cross a footbridge and continue ahead on a green lane.

When this meets a minor road, continue on the footpath which goes through a narrow gap next to a telegraph pole. Beyond the garden, continue across a field to a concrete bridge, crossing the next field half-right, to a foot bridge in the field corner. Turn left to go along the left side of a field, turning right in the field corner. Look out for a footbridge on the left; cross it, turn right, and continue with a ditch on right. Cross the main road (B184), turn left, and just before the school turn right on a track, which takes you towards the church at **Great Easton**.

Great Easton occupies a spur above the Chelmer, with a single street running down to the river from the church. The grounds of Great Easton Hall, down the lane to the left, include the remains of a motte and

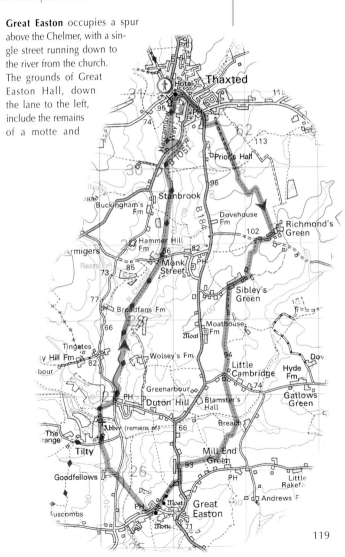

119

bailey. The Swan Inn is one of many listed buildings to admire.

From the war memorial, take the footpath (numbered 5) between houses on the right. After the second stile, cross the field half-left over two footbridges (the second is over the Chelmer), to a minor road, where you turn right. At the farm drive, take the footpath heading half-left to a stile. Proceed across a field, the spire of Thaxted church in the distance, and much closer, the tiny church at **Tilty**.

> Tilty was once the site of a great **Cistercian abbey**; the church was then its gatehouse chapel. Look for the enormous east window and the high ceiling with original 12th-century beams. King John lived up to his bad reputation here, post-Magna Carta, sacking the abbey during Christmas mass in 1215.

Continue through a kissing gate, the abbey ruins on your right, to the derelict Tilty Mill. Keep it on your left and take the track leading past a pillbox disguised under an iron roof. At a marker turn right on a path which comes out at a minor road junction at **Duton Hill**: cross the bridge over the Chelmer, but just after it take the footpath on the left, through a garden. **The Three Horseshoes** is in the village a short distance along the road.

From the garden keep the Chelmer close by on your left almost all the way to Thaxted, around two miles. There's just one road to be crossed, at Follymill. Eventually, the **B1051** comes in from the left – where it does so, the Chelmer heads north, while a side stream separates you from the road for 200 metres, until you can cross a footbridge to it. Turn left back along the road, cross it, and after Park Style Cottage turn right on a path which climbs towards the attractive grouping of windmill and church. In the churchyard keep the church on your left, and return to the Guildhall down the cobbled Stoney Lane.

Beside the Chelmer north of Duton Hill

THAXTED

The large church and fine Guildhall attest to the long-standing importance of this attractive little town. Both buildings date from the 14th century, and owe their construction to an unexpected source of wealth – the medieval cutlery industry, which was to flourish here for well over 200 years.

The town had been important since Saxon times, with a formal market charter granted in 1205. The Dick Turpin connection, alluded to by the naming of a house for him on Stoney Lane, is alas more likely to be mythic than real.

Just as colourful was the radical Rev Conrad Noel, vicar from 1910, who flew the red and Sinn Féin flags from the church and, keen to encourage the arts, attracted Gustav Holst to the town. The composer founded the first music festivals here; after Noel died in 1942, Holst student Jack Putteril became vicar, continuing the musical tradition.

WALK 21
Finchingfield and Great Bardfield

Start/Finish	Finchingfield war memorial (TL 684 328); on busy days, parking can be a nightmare in Finchingfield, and it is better to start at the Great Bardfield war memorial (TL 676 305)
Distance	5½ miles (9km)
Walking time	2½hr
Maps	OS Explorer 195, Landranger 167
Refreshments	Many options in both Finchingfield and Great Bardfield
Public transport	Buses from Braintree and Chelmsford (not Sundays)

Let them come to Finchingfield, those who believe that Essex has no picturesque. The setting of duckpond, church and windmill, eulogised on a thousand chocolate boxes, draws hundreds on sunny days, but fewer venture to nearby Great Bardfield: a shame, for although very different, it's scarcely less good, full to the brim of homes of architectural merit, several dating to its medieval days as a market town. This walk links the two by the valleys of the infant River Pant and the Finchingfield Brook.

From the war memorial, take the Saffron Walden road uphill. Turn right on a footpath at 'Molen' and turn left when you come out to a minor road. Soon the great Elizabethan house of Spain's Hall comes into view. ◀ Opposite its drive, turn left on the track to **Darielay Farm**. Veer left after passing the house, at a junction continue ahead into a wood, and when the track comes out to a road, turn left. In 100 metres turn right onto a bridleway, which becomes a green lane after a spinney; when it ends, turn left onto a farm road.

The 'Spain' of the title is the same Norman baron who gave his name to one of the Willingale parishes (see *Across Essex*, Stage 3).

Keep ahead towards Great Bardfield at a road junction and in 100 metres turn right over a stile. The stream in the dip is the River Pant; when you reach it, turn left over a stile, keeping the river on your right until just past a farm, and then cross a footbridge. Continue with the river on your left, leaving the left side of a field at a marker. After an area of saplings, the path heads between fences, over a footbridge and through scrub, following a marker left through a gap to a gate, which leads to the car park of the **Vine** pub at Great Bardfield.

Great Bardfield was home to its own art movement in the middle of the last century, with a dozen or so artists resident here of whom Edward Bawden and Eric Ravilious are perhaps the best-known. Bawden's lithographs for Penguin, *Life in an English Village*, are an important record of rural life in the 1940s. Modernist but figurative (unlike the contemporane-ous St Ives artists), the movement culminated with a series of showings in the artists' homes during the mid and late 1950s. The village bookshop has many volumes about their work. More recently, Turner prize-winner Grayson Perry lived here as a young boy and had a newspaper round; see Stage 11 of the Essex Way for an example of his work. There is also a village museum, open weekends, on Bridge Street; it includes the village lock-up, known as the Cage.

Flax crop north of Finchingfield

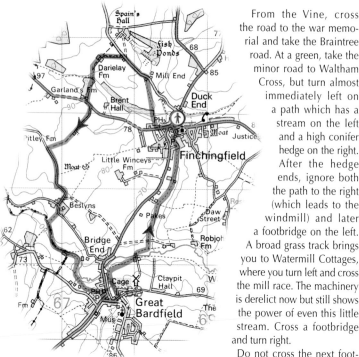

From the Vine, cross the road to the war memorial and take the Braintree road. At a green, take the minor road to Waltham Cross, but turn almost immediately left on a path which has a stream on the left and a high conifer hedge on the right. After the hedge ends, ignore both the path to the right (which leads to the windmill) and later a footbridge on the left. A broad grass track brings you to Watermill Cottages, where you turn left and cross the mill race. The machinery is derelict now but still shows the power of even this little stream. Cross a footbridge and turn right.

Do not cross the next footbridge; instead turn left, with the ditch on your right, soon switching when you cross a farm track to have the ditch on your left, as shown by a marker. The ditch moves away but you soon come to Finchingfield Brook; keep this close by on your right for about a kilometre. The path becomes fenced in but with a lovely view of Finchingfield **church** across a meadow. At a metalled path, turn right across a footbridge and go up a grassy bank to the churchyard. Leave the churchyard by steps beside the Guildhall arch, and turn left onto the road back down to the start.

WALK 22

Castle Hedingham and Hull's Mill

Start/Finish	Bayley Street, Castle Hedingham, outside the castle entrance (TL 786 357); parking is also available inside the castle grounds when it is open, free with castle admission charge, but check you have time to finish the walk before the grounds close
Distance	7 miles (11km)
Walking time	3hr
Maps	OS Explorer 195. Landranger not recommended – 155, 167 and 168 are all needed
Refreshments	Bell and Wheatsheaf pubs and Buckley's tea rooms in the village; café in the castle
Public transport	Buses from Braintree (not Sundays)

This walk links three contrasted sites of Norman heritage – the castle, the church at Great Maplestead, and a successor of the Norman mills of the River Colne – by way of Dyne's Park and the tranquil river itself. Castle Hedingham village, saved for the end of the walk, is a gem: a cluster of colourful streets, with buildings from the imposing (on Queen Street, the main entrance to the village) to the delightful (Churchponds).

Walk ahead along Bayley Street with the castle grounds on your left and continue out of the village. Past New Park, take the first footpath on the right, which at a telegraph pole forks half-left across a field into a dip below Little Lodge Farm. Turn left onto the field headland, then right along the farm lane. At the first farm outhouses, turn left, and turn half-right immediately past the last of these (lettered E), joining a path at an oak tree and keeping to the left edge of a field to its corner. Here, you cross an earth bridge, turn right, and then in 20 metres turn left on a grass strip across a field.

Where this finishes turn right on a track, and just past a solitary house take the footpath heading left by a hedgerow. This soon ends; then, trend very slightly left across the field to a marker and continue. In the dip ahead go through the kissing gate on your right (or, if it is overgrown, the farm gate a few yards further on), continuing with a ditch on your right. After a little wood there is a fox-proof enclosure where game chicks are raised. About 50 metres after this, the path heads left up steps, turning right at the top. You eventually enter **Great Maplestead** (quite legally!) through the back garden of 1 Stone Cottages. Enter St Giles churchyard ahead.

The **church** replaced a pagan chapel on the site in about 1100 and boasts aisle and transept on both north and south sides, the former being deliberately added by the Victorians in the name of balance. Off the south transept is the Deane (later Dyne) family chapel (1626) – the walk soon passes through what was the family estate.

At the back of the churchyard, go through a gap to the

right of the Cuddeford memorial. From here a path leads very slightly right downhill across a field – look for the marker over the field. When you reach it, go down steps and follow the left edge of a field into a willow plantation. Some 50 metres along, turn left over a footbridge and up the hill. Near the top, keep the fence on your left, coming out to a road at a T-junction. Continue ahead along Mill Lane, and at **Mill Farm** turn right on a footpath at a concrete sign.

Dyne's Hall Park

Immediately after an earth bridge, turn left. The right-of-way crosses the open field towards a water trough; most walkers find it easier to take the headland of the field, with the stream on the left. ▶ Both variants come to a footbridge. Once across, continue to a minor road. Turn right onto the road, passing the drive to **Dyne's Hall**, and leave it at a track into woodland on the left.

The parkland you are passing through is used for national-standard eventing competitions.

Some 200 metres past the derelict **Wallace's Farm**, take the footpath left at a tree-belt. Turn right where it meets the old railway embankment. Soon you pick up Colne Valley Path waymarkers and reach **Hull's Mill**.

There was a **mill** on this site since at least the Domesday book records of 1086. The present building, which dates from 1848, was brought by the Hovis company in 1917, and provided grain for its famous loaves – then as now baked in metropolitan Essex at Forest Gate – until its closure in 1957. The cottages just over the ford were provided for millworkers.

Cross the Colne by ford or footbridge and turn right through a kissing gate, soon keeping to the river until a ditch forces you left. Go through the metal kissing gate; 100 metres later turn right over an earth bridge, and continue ahead, ignoring footpaths to the left. You come out at Alderford Mill, which like Hull's Mill continued in use to the late 1950s. ◀

Alderford Mill is in public hands, in course of restoration, and occasionally open to the public.

HEDINGHAM CASTLE

The castle was built around 1140 for one of the most powerful Norman families, the de Veres, later the Earls of Oxford. It was a remarkable statement of power: the facing stonework alone, transported from Northamptonshire, cost a quarter of the annual budget

of the royal household itself, and the 28ft arch spanning the great hall exceeds any other Norman arch, cathedrals included.

The castle surrendered after sieges in 1216 and 1217, in retribution for the earl being a signatory of Magna Carta, but the family remained at the centre of royal life for centuries more. Descendants of the de Veres still own the castle today.

The formal garden surrounding the 'Queen Anne' house dates from 1715; its 20th-century neglect was reversed in 2009 as a project for the Channel 4 programme 'The Landscape Man'. The castle and grounds are open sporadically from April to October: check www.hedinghamcastle.co.uk.

Turn right on the road, cross the river, and after an old railway bridge turn left, still on the Colne Valley Path. After leaving a small farmyard, turn left at a marker on a path with impressively lush vegetation to the left. Just before you reach a road, there is a sudden view of the castle beyond. At the road, turn right up to **Castle Hedingham** village. There are many enchanting ways through the village, but a good choice (which alas omits the 15th-century Bell Inn on St James Street) is to turn left onto King Street at the Wheatsheaf, into Falcon Square, left into Churchponds, and then continue along Crown Street to Bayley Street, where turn right to complete the walk.

WALK 23
Chalkney Wood and Earl's Colne

Start/Finish	Chappel & Wakes Colne station (TL 897 288)
Distance	8 miles (13km) or 4½ miles (7km)
Walking time	3½hr; 2hr for the shorter route
Maps	OS Explorer 195, Landranger 168
Refreshments	Café in the museum at the station; Swan pub at Chappel; three pubs in Earl's Colne, as well as tea rooms and restaurants
Public transport	The station is on the Marks Tey–Sudbury branch line. Buses from Colchester travel along the A1124

Although not one of the most wooded counties, Essex has plenty of areas of fine forest. This walk takes in one of them, Chalkney Wood, which sits on a bank overlooking the River Colne. After visiting the busy village of Earl's Colne, the return by the river skirts the base of the wood. And on the way out there's a close look at the most notable piece of railway architecture in East Anglia, the Colne Valley Viaduct.

Walk down the station access road and turn left down Station Road. The museum at the station is open daily, but check in advance for days when there are engines in steam. Cross the A1124 and turn left. Just before the viaduct, turn right on a footpath beside it, cross the Colne and immediately go underneath the viaduct.

> **Chappel Viaduct** was the largest brick structure in England when completed in 1847, and has since been surpassed only by Battersea Power Station. Unlike the power station, it is still used for its original purpose. Each of the 32 arches has a 30ft span, the highest rising 75ft over the river.

Keep ahead by the railway line to a footbridge. Here, cross a field, aiming just to the right of the house at **Pope's Hall**. By the house, turn right on a lane, leading back under the railway. Turn left where it meets a road; follow this past Knights Farm to the hamlet of **Swan Street**, and take the footpath right up steps opposite the first thatched cottage. Across a footbridge in the dip, this rises through a field and later down steps to a junction of minor roads to your left. Take the right fork, which is the drive to Priory House. Beyond the house (kept on your right), the drive is a footpath, and beyond stables a green lane. At a path crossroads, turn left across a field, past a pond, through a gate, and over

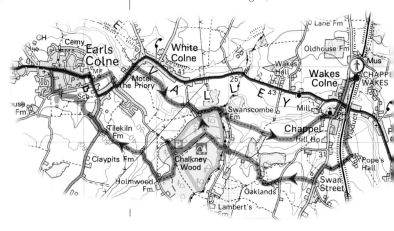

a footbridge to a minor road. Turn right on this and then almost immediately left to enter **Chalkney Wood**.

Snow beside the Colne

> There is public access throughout **Chalkney Wood**, the northern and eastern parts owned by the Forestry Commission and the south-western by the county council. The now rare small-leaved lime dominates the latter portion; as conifers are harvested in the Forestry Commission area, native species are being allowed to grow through.

Walk ahead into the wood on the path, ignoring the first broad path on your left, until you come to the meeting point of your path with three others; a footpath coming in from the right and three broad tracks.

Shorter route
For the shorter walk take the broad track heading half-right; this soon brings you to the farmyard at Chalkney

Earl's Colne

Mill, where turn right after the cowshed to join the route described below.

Take the central track, heading slightly left. Eventually this narrows to a footpath and comes out to a sanded **car park** in a clearing. Walk ahead through the car park, as if you were to leave the forest, but without doing so turn sharp left at a waymark on a wooden post, taking the broader of the two paths (that is, the one not heading back beside the car park). Another footpath marker soon confirms your direction, and at a second marker by a bench take the right turn.

Leave the forest at a minor road, where turn right downhill to a pylon. Here, a concrete sign points ahead, but in fact you should enter the field on your left and keep the hedge on your right. After a short rise, continue with the hedge on your left. Cross the B1024, go ahead past houses, and at a bend go ahead on the path marked by a concrete signpost. Go through a metal kissing gate on your right, cross the meadow to go through a gate, and fork downhill, joining a boardwalk. Turn right just before it finishes and walk through Long Meadow. ◀ Leave it at

The meadow, rich in species such as bird's-foot trefoil, is part of a local nature reserve.

a gate and turn right, then left when you come to Park Lane in **Earl's Colne**.

> As with Castle Hedingham (Walk 22), **Earl's Colne** was a settlement in the tract of land granted by William the Conqueror to his brother-in-law Aubrey de Vere; the abbey became the estate's principal religious site, as the castle became its central fortification. Victorian industry came here in 1885 through the agricultural machinery factory of R Hunt & Co, which survived for more than a century; the town's story is told in a museum sited there. Although close to the town of Halstead, Earl's Colne retains a wide variety of shops and places for refreshment.

Turn right into Foundry Lane, past the old factory, and right again to walk down the High Street. At the end of this enter the **churchyard** through one lych gate and leave it by another. Cross over Church Hill and take the concrete path leading away from the main road, with a cemetery on your right. Turn right at metal gates. ▶ Continue to the A1124 and turn left. After crossing the Colne, take the first footpath on the right beside house 22. The path joins the Colne at a kissing gate and stays beside or close to it to a pylon, where you turn right and walk past Chalkney Mill.

This is the site of the former Benedictine priory, the last fragment (a tower) surviving to 1988.

Turn left in the farmyard to follow a path which runs below Chalkney Wood. A high wooden fence and brick wall hide what is called **Swanscombe Farm**; at the house, turn right on the drive, but leave it soon, at a footpath through a gate which crosses a field slightly right. This continues through a gate and a footbridge to but not through a gate in a hedgerow. Continue with the hedge on your right, across a footbridge at a pond, through an area of saplings, and proceed to Chappel **church**, then turn left back to the station.

RAILWAYS OF ESSEX

The Colne Valley Viaduct

The viaduct at Chappel is an anomaly: the geography of Essex did not generally make life difficult for the Victorian railway engineer. Indeed, until the Central Line extended eastwards there were only four tunnels in the entire county, two near Audley End where the diversion to avoid the estate meant cutting through the chalk hills to its north. The others were a short stretch of the North Woolwich branch underneath the Royal Docks, now closed but due to reopen as part of the Crossrail project, and one near Chigwell.

The very first Essex town to be linked to London was Romford, in 1839; the main lines to Cambridge and Ipswich, familiar to this day, were completed seven years later. Some of the branch lines arrived surprisingly late. Clacton had to wait until 1882 for its link, and the lines either side of the Crouch estuary were not complete until later in that decade. A couple – to Tollesbury and Thaxted – did not arrive until the early 20th century.

The Eastern Counties company, later (1862) the Great Eastern Railway, promoted most of the lines, but the London, Tilbury and Southend system (from 1854) was always independent of it and indeed remains distinct. The blue-liveried engines of the Great Eastern were almost all built at the vast works at Stratford, which in 1891 set a new record of building an entire locomotive in less than ten hours.

The 1950s and 1960s saw many branches close, Tollesbury and Thaxted first, then the Colne Valley and Braintree to Bishop's Stortford lines. Three towns suffered due to the Beeching cuts: Brightlingsea, Saffron Walden and Maldon. The Ongar branch of the Central line closed in 1994. But recently there has been growth too, all of it needing the tunnels that the Victorians could avoid: Stansted Airport in 1991, the HS1 channel tunnel link (2007), and in metropolitan Essex – specifically the borough of Newham – the Docklands Light Railway (1987 onwards).

WALK 24
Bures to Sudbury

Start	Bures railway station (TL 903 339), free parking
Finish	Sudbury railway station (TL 876 410)
Distance	7½ miles (12km)
Walking time	3½hr
Maps	Explorer 196, Landranger 155 (first few metres on 168)
Refreshments	Eight Bells pub in Bures, Lion at Lamarsh en route, and many alternatives in Sudbury
Public transport	The start and finish are both on the Marks Tey to Sudbury branch line; note that Bures is a request stop. Bures is also served by the Colchester–Sudbury bus (not Sundays)

This walk takes advantage of the excellent Sudbury branch line and the Stour Valley Path, a long-distance trail from Manningtree to Newmarket. The village of Bures straddles the Stour and so has always been split into Suffolk and Essex halves; the walk keeps resolutely to the Essex side to explore the little side valleys that feed the river before crossing the county boundary for the final mile. Never mind that Sudbury is just in Suffolk; it's a historic town, the birthplace of Thomas Gainsborough.

From the station in Bures, turn right out of The Paddocks and at the bottom of Station Hill turn left on the footpath shown by the concrete sign. This soon becomes a track with

135

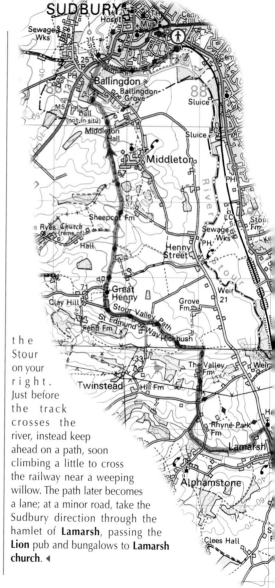

the Stour on your right. Just before the track crosses the river, instead keep ahead on a path, soon climbing a little to cross the railway near a weeping willow. The path later becomes a lane; at a minor road, take the Sudbury direction through the hamlet of **Lamarsh**, passing the **Lion** pub and bungalows to **Lamarsh church**. ◄

With its round Norman tower – one of only three in the country, and capped with a Victorian spire – the church looks more French than Essex.

136

The **Stour Valley Path**, followed (with the St Edmund's Way) this far from Bures, now heads over a rather dull patch of tableland. Better instead to keep to one of the Stour's side valleys for a while. Opposite the church, take the footpath heading uphill, turning left at a marker near the top and then in 50 metres right at the next marker. Keep ahead, the side valley sloping away on your left. You come to a very minor road where you have a choice. One is to turn right uphill on the road; the other is to cross it and continue, ignoring a broken stile but soon veering up to a gate. Through the gate, continue to another very minor road and turn right uphill – but on the way you will have to scale a waist-high wire (not barbed) fence strung across the right-of-way. The two very minor roads merge and come to a T-junction. Here, regain the Stour Valley Path at the gate ahead.

Drop slightly right through a grass field to a way-marked gate in the right corner. Turn left on the lane, pass **Valley Farm** on your left, and cross a pair of footbridges. Head up through a field; at the top, do not go through the gate, but turn left, eventually joining the lane serving the large house which appears on your left. Follow this to a minor road and turn left towards **Great Henny church**, finally reaching it on a lane after a brown weatherboarded house. ▸

From the lych gate, take the path heading away, beside the Old Hatchery. Just past a farm, cross the stile on the left. Continue to the next stile, cross it and turn right, and cross a footbridge. From here there are many ups and downs as the north-heading path crosses side streams of the Stour; markers show the way whenever there is a chance of doubt. After the grassy parkland of a dry valley, the great church at Long Melford is clearly in sight. Eventually, you cross part

The oak spire of the church was reclad in 2000 following continual hammering from the beaks of woodpeckers calling for mates.

Distant view to Long Melford

of a field to a hedge gap and enter Suffolk for the last mile of the walk.

Keep between hedgerows into a wooded area, go through a play area, and turn left on the estate road beyond. Where this ends, cross over into Kone Vale, and take the obvious path ahead to reach the old railway embankment. Take the ramp on the left leading up to it and turn right onto the old railway. You cross over two bridges, the first over the Stour and the second at the town quay. Pass the Waitrose car park and **Sudbury station** is just the other side of the leisure centre in front of you. Alternatively, to visit the town, turn left after the second bridge and then immediately right, turn left past garages, and continue over the road to Friars Street. Turn right here for the Market Hill.

WALK 25
Dedham

Start/Finish	Manningtree station (TM 094 322)
Distance	7 miles (11km)
Walking time	3hr
Maps	Explorer 196, Landranger 168
Refreshments	Manningtree station refreshment room; café at Flatford Mill; pubs and cafés in Dedham
Public transport	Rail services to Manningtree

No Essex walker should miss Dedham, a town worthy of its fame even without the Constable connection. This walk takes the south bank of the Stour past Flatford Mill into Dedham itself, before using the Essex Way to head uphill to Lawford's beautiful church.

The bridge at Flatford Mill

Turn right out of **Manningtree station** and within a few
yards you will see the footpath sign for Flatford. After a
metalled stretch by the railway, the path goes under the
line and heads for the banks of the Stour. Stay beside or
close to the river, passing the **Flatford Mill** immortalised
by Constable, until, at a double gate, the path leaves the
riverbank and heads into Dedham. Although you stay on
the south bank of the Stour, the mile around the mill is
in Suffolk, for the county boundary follows the course of
Dedham Old River.

From Dedham war memorial to Lawford church, the
walk follows the **Essex Way**. Pass the Duchy Barn and
turn right behind the cricket pavilion. Before you reach
the end of the boundary, turn left through a kissing gate.
Just past a footbridge, turn half-left at a marker, and over
another footbridge, walk up to and past the pink house
ahead. Turn right on a minor road, then left on an (initially) gravel track just past 'Hunter's Moon'. The Way
eventually crosses a meadow to turn right onto a road.
Turn left onto Anchor Lane for 30 metres and then keep
ahead to a minor road, where you turn right for 250
metres. Turn left through a gap with a kissing gate,
cross half-right to a minor road, and go over,
through paddocks to the main railway
line. Cross this with care, making
sure you can neither
see nor hear
any trains.

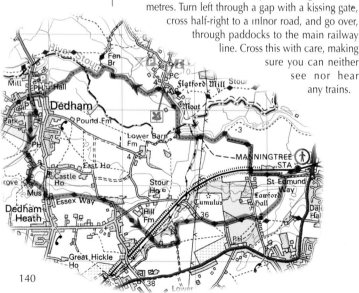

DEDHAM

Like Coggeshall (Across Essex, Stage 6), Dedham grew rich on the wool and later cloth trades, and its merchants built great houses – most still standing – to demonstrate their wealth. For their sons, a grammar school was established in 1575, and this helped maintain the importance of the town as the wool trade declined.

Two hundred years later, it was natural for Golding Constable to send his son John to the school. Golding, a wealthy East Bergholt corn merchant, owned Flatford Mill, half way to Dedham. And now, it's difficult to move in Dedham for references to 'Constable Country'.

It is, of course, immensely rewarding to trace the locations favoured by the great Romantic painter and to find them so untouched two centuries on. Indeed, this walk and the Essex Way from Langham to Lawford give a fine introduction to many of his favoured viewpoints. But Constable connections only scrape the surface of what Dedham and its environs have to offer. In art alone, it was also home to Sir Alfred Munnings, the greatest English horse-painter since Stubbs, and Tom Keating, perhaps the most effective art forger ever. The East Anglian School of Painting and Drawing, which Lucien Freud attended as a young man, was set up here in 1937.

Dedham was also important in the growth of Puritanism in the 17th century, the popularity of lectures by preachers such as John Rogers drawing from miles around those open to new views of religion. The town was strongly parliamentarian in the Civil War.

Manningtree station buffet

Go into a wood over a plank bridge. At 'Slumberlands' the Essex Way follows a lane to 'Broom Knolls', where through a gate you turn right, and later right onto a road. Beside 'The Lodge', turn left through a wooden gate onto a gravel track. Go through a kissing gate on your right, heading to another; St Mary the Virgin church at **Lawford** is just beyond.

Enter the churchyard at the church sign, passing the new church hall on your right. Beyond, the path takes a pleasant course between hedgerows before heading downhill to Manningtree station.

HERE ENDS THE

ESSEX WAY

81 FOOTPATH MILES

FROM EPPING

COUNCIL FOR THE PROTECTION OF RURAL ESSEX

CAMPAIGN FOR THE COUNTRYSIDE

The end of the Essex Way

The 11 stages described in this section cross the county from Manor Park, on the fringes of London, to the port of Harwich – a distance of 96 miles (154km). The first 15 of these miles traverse Epping Forest, and the rest are on the Essex Way. There's an immense satisfaction to be had from a long linear walk like this, with a clear objective in mind, and seeing so many of the characteristics of the county unveil themselves as you continue onwards.

The Essex Way was the first of the modern long-distance paths in the county, developed by Fred Matthews and Harry Bitten of the West Essex Ramblers' Association in 1971; indeed, it was also one of the first county LDPs. They later set up many more paths in the county (see Appendix C), including the Epping Forest Centenary Walk, celebrating the centenary of the Epping Forest Act, which safeguarded it from enclosure.

Stage 1 follows the Centenary Walk closely but not precisely; the original route has not been revised since publication, and some sections can now be tricky to follow. Explorer maps show the exact line for those who wish to follow it. By contrast the Essex Way is very well waymarked, and so the route directions which follow are a little less detailed than elsewhere.

A long linear walk needs more forethought than a short circular one. First of all, do you want to undertake it in one go or a bit at a time? It's often people who live locally who will do the route as and when they can. You'll need to know how many miles a day you are comfortable with, and then find suitable break points. In this guide, the longer sections can themselves be broken, for example the Epping Forest stage at Chingford and Dedham-to-Wrabness at Mistley; but equally, many long-distance walkers find that 15 miles or even more gives a good day out, so will be combining stages.

All the stages break at places with good public transport, at least hourly during the day although perhaps not Sundays, although slightly fewer for Dedham. Assuming there is no willing volunteer to leave you at the start and pick you up at the finish, the alternative is the two-car shuffle, which is how the author first walked the route 30 years ago. More recently, all the research for this part of the book used public transport from east London, so it can be done.

Purest of all is to walk the route in one go, either from a central base – Chelmsford would be good – or, in the classic fashion, with overnight accommodation in the villages along the way. The latter is the ideal, but needs careful thought. Some accommodation options are suggested at the beginning of each route description, but it's also worth checking for alternatives either from the web or via Tourist Information Centres.

STAGE 1

Manor Park to Epping

Start	Manor Park station (TQ 418 856), parking nearby on Capel Road (TQ 418 859)
Finish	Epping station (TL 462 015)
Distance	14½ miles (23km); it can be split into two halves by breaking at Chingford
Walking time	6hr (or two 3hr walks)
Maps	OS Explorer 174, Landranger 177/167
Refreshments	Golden Fleece near the start; Royal Forest Inn and Butler's Retreat café at Chingford; King's Oak Hotel and tea huts at High Beach; Forest Gate Inn at Bell Common
Public transport	Rail to start, Central line from finish
Accommodation	Premier Inn Chingford (TQ 396 947, on stage, Tel 0871 527 9386, www.premierinn.com), The Gate House (TL 450 011, on stage, Tel 01992 578052, https://stayinepping.co.uk)

Epping Forest sits on a gravel ridge between two major tributaries of the Thames, the Roding and Lea. This walk, based on that created in 1978 to honour the centenary of the passing of the Epping Forest Act, traverses the present Forest from its southern almost to its northern extremity, and makes a fine excursion: from the open spaces at the edge of the inner city to the great trees of the high forest.

With **Manor Park station** on your left, walk along the main road to Capel Road. Here, take the path shown by white posts heading half-left onto **Wanstead Flats**, the southernmost part of Epping Forest land. At Alexandra Pond, head roughly towards

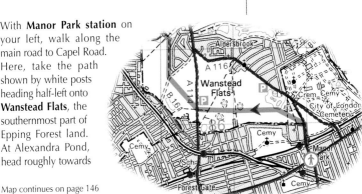

Map continues on page 146

Winter in Bush Wood

Map continues on
page 148

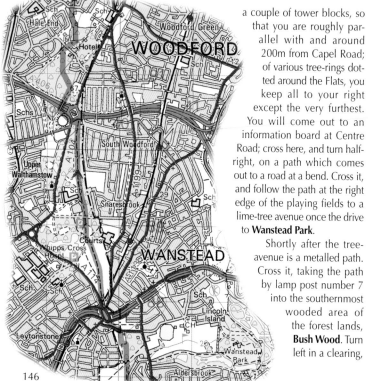

a couple of tower blocks, so
that you are roughly par-
allel with and around
200m from Capel Road;
of various tree-rings dot-
ted around the Flats, you
keep all to your right
except the very furthest.
You will come out to an
information board at Centre
Road; cross here, and turn half-
right, on a path which comes
out to a road at a bend. Cross it,
and follow the path at the right
edge of the playing fields to a
lime-tree avenue once the drive
to **Wanstead Park**.

Shortly after the tree-
avenue is a metalled path.
Cross it, taking the path
by lamp post number 7
into the southernmost
wooded area of
the forest lands,
Bush Wood. Turn
left in a clearing,

WANSTEAD PARK

Wanstead Park was once one of the grandest houses and estates, not simply of Essex, but of England. Its loss results from an unfortunate marriage.

At the end of the 15th century, this area of the Essex forest was enclosed for royal sport. Later, Elizabeth I's favourite Robert Dudley replaced the hunting lodge with a new house, and entertained her there. After the restoration, Sir Josiah Child, governor of the East India company and a self-made man, oversaw the first formal garden design, with walnut trees and fishponds; in 1715, his son Richard started work on a grand Palladian mansion that would rival Blenheim.

A century later, the estate had passed to Catherine Tylney-Long, at 21 the richest heiress in England. Marriage to William Wellesley-Pole, nephew of the Duke of Wellington, must have made perfect sense at the time. He had, alas, eyes less for his bride than her money, and as one of the most notorious Regency rakes could find plenty of uses for the latter. After ten years of marriage in 1822, the contents of the house had to be sold off for debtors; two years later, the house itself was demolished for the value of its materials, there being no buyers for the house intact; and within months, Catherine was dead at 35.

Most of the park has been part of Epping Forest lands since the 1878 Act, but the site of the house itself sits on a private golf course.

branch right before houses, and turn left along Bush Road, using the pelican crossing to take the pedestrian route through two underpasses and over a railway bridge. Here you enter Leyton Flats. Take the path by a white-topped post, veer right in 100 metres, go through a copse, and in another 70 metres take the right fork. Just before the next tree belt, veer left to avoid going through it. Over to your right appear the cupolas of **Snaresbrook Crown Court**, where many an East End villain has faced judgement. Join a larger path, go between ponds, then veer right and you will come out at the car park for Leyton Flats.

Continue on the path over the road; housing, and then the private Forest School, appear on your left. In a clearing after the school, keep ahead. Go through an underpass, keep left under a second underpass, then immediately go up a little bank. The large circle of grass

Map continues on
page 150

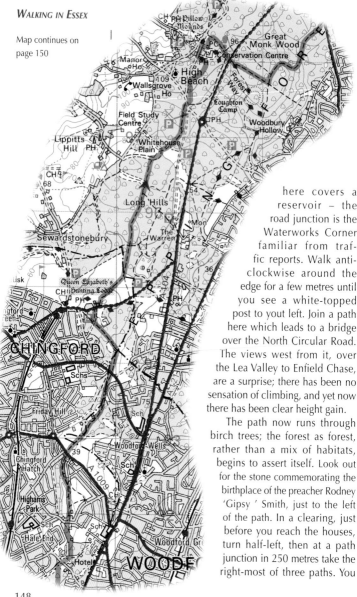

here covers a
reservoir – the
road junction is the
Waterworks Corner
familiar from traf-
fic reports. Walk anti-
clockwise around the
edge for a few metres until
you see a white-topped
post to yout left. Join a path
here which leads to a bridge
over the North Circular Road.
The views west from it, over
the Lea Valley to Enfield Chase,
are a surprise; there has been no
sensation of climbing, and yet now
there has been clear height gain.

The path now runs through
birch trees; the forest as forest,
rather than a mix of habitats,
begins to assert itself. Look out
for the stone commemorating the
birthplace of the preacher Rodney
'Gipsy ' Smith, just to the left
of the path. In a clearing, just
before you reach the houses,
turn half-left, then at a path
junction in 250 metres take the
right-most of three paths. You

Queen Elizabeth's Hunting Lodge

meet a row of semi-detached houses, which you keep on your left. Cross Oak Hill, taking the narrower path at an unmade parking area. When you reach **Highams Park Lake**, keep it on your left, and beyond its head, keep the little Ching Brook to your left as well. Eventually you head a little uphill to a road.

Over some scrub there is a **golf course**, but you only cross one fairway; beyond it, fork left then left again. Cross Whitehall Road, and in 300 metres turn left over an earth bridge. Warren Pond appears on your right, and beyond it you come to **Queen Elizabeth's Hunting Lodge**, with the **Royal Forest Inn** and Butler's Retreat café either side. ▶ If you are breaking the walk here, **Chingford train station** is about half a kilometre to your left along the main road.

The hunting lodge was built in 1543 so that royals could view hunts from the then-open top storeys: open afternoons except Monday and Tuesday.

From Butler's Retreat, take the path leading downhill from a drinking fountain (not the path by a small pond). Continue ahead (not right) when it becomes a hard-surfaced ride, which you follow for about a mile and a half. Crossing a road that has a tea hut on the right, do not continue on the ride but turn left on a path near the road. Veer right behind buildings, cross a clearing, and reaching a fence, turn left beside it, then right on a road at the **King's Oak Hotel** in High Beach. It's worth crossing the

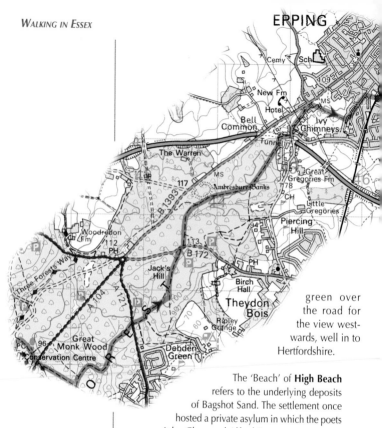

green over the road for the view westwards, well in to Hertfordshire.

The 'Beach' of **High Beach** refers to the underlying deposits of Bagshot Sand. The settlement once hosted a private asylum in which the poets John Clare and Alfred Tennyson were once residents, and possibly met. In 1928, the area of the visitor centre hosted the first motorcycle speedway meeting in Britain, and motorcycle pilgrimages are still very popular here.

Turn right after the pub, through its car park, and take the 'easy access' path just by a large 'welcome' sign. The visitor centre here is open from Thursdays to Sundays. Turn right just before a little pond, then right again. Ignore a left fork, but leave the ride soon after on a thin path heading through a fence down to the A104. Cross over, to a

gate which has a **Forest Way** marker. At a coppiced beech tree 100 metres along the path turn left then in a few yards right, veering slightly left through a clearing; the path then becomes indistinct, so look out for cycle tracks and similar evidence. Meeting a ride, turn left: this is Green Ride, cut for Queen Victoria's visit in 1882, but alas never used by her due to the inclement weather. Today, it will take you three miles to the outskirts of Epping; it keeps to the eastern side of the escarpment, indented by streams falling down to the Roding, so has a bit more up-and-down than the walk so far.

Soon after joining Green Ride, ignore a left fork. The ride crosses two roads, at Golding's Hill (bus stop for Loughton tube if needed!) and Jack's Hill. Look out for the initial left turn after the former and ignore the ride coming in from the right in between them. About half a mile after **Jack's Hill**, ignore a ride on the left; soon, the earthworks of **Ambresbury Banks Iron Age hill fort**, yet another mythic site for Boudicca's last stand, are to the left. Ignore a right-heading ride, and at the next path

Ambresbury Banks

junction, keep ahead to a common. Turn right, then at a road left, then right past the Forest Gate Inn.

You are on **Bell Common**, the site of a real (but bloodless) conflict. The Common gives its name to the tunnel which here carries the M25 beneath the forest. The original intention was to slice a cutting, but the proposal was defeated by popular outrage. Alas, as South Downs Way walkers will know, cost-benefit people had an ugly revenge with the desecration of Twyford Down by the M3.

Keep on past all the houses, cross over the lane that leads to Hemnall House, follow a path heading right. (For Epping's High Street, instead walk along the main road a few yards away on your left.) Keep on the right edge of a meadow and continue half-left on a green lane. Turn left onto a suburban road and left again. Just past Woodland Grove, take the path on the right to Epping Station.

ENCLOSURE OF LAND

Common land in England had been subject to enclosure, often for sheep-farming, since the Middle Ages, but the advent of 'Parliamentary enclosure' from 1773 prevented local people from continuing practices (from cultivation to fishing) in enclosed areas that their forebears had carried out for centuries. Around 20 per cent of England's land was enclosed, most of it within 50 years.

Epping Forest was by no means exempt. Indeed it might be said that the loss of Royal protection of the Forest as hunting ground emboldened local landlords to enclose; by 1871 12,000 unenclosed 'waste' acres had been reduced to 2000. The loss of grazing rights was universally missed, but in the Loughton area, the loss of 'lopping rights' for winter wood-fuel was particularly resented. In 1864 the local Lord of the Manor, Rev Maitland, enclosed 1300 acres of forest land, in part with a view to property development – the railway had opened in 1856. Villager Thomas Willingale, already a noted opponent of enclosure, tackled this directly, openly lopping on the newly-enclosed land; he was prosecuted, and others of his family were imprisoned.

Willingale was not short of support. As east and north London pressed their boundaries ever closer, the new population valued the chance of recreation in the unpolluted Forest. This case coincided with the establishment of the Commons Preservation Society by the likes of William Morris, JS Mill and Edward North Buxton of Leytonstone (later to buy Hatfield Forest for the nation). Crucially, the City of London Corporation, through Council member John T Bedford, became sympathetic.

A year after Willingale's death in 1870, local people took direct action against the enclosure of Wanstead Flats by pulling down fences there, and the City commenced legal action against the lords of several manors. The case was successful, and led directly to the Epping Forest Act of 1878, under which the Conservators 'shall at all times keep Epping Forest unincosed and unbuilt on, as an open space for the recreation and enjoyment of the public'.

STAGE 2
Epping to Ongar

Start	Epping station (TL 462 015)
Finish	Budworth Hall, Ongar (TL 552 031)
Distance	7½ miles (12km)
Walking time	3½hr
Maps	OS Explorer 174/183, Landranger 167
Refreshments	Theydon Oak at Coopersale Street; Green Man at Toot Hill; pubs and cafés in Ongar
Public transport	Central line and local buses to Epping; buses from Ongar back to Epping, and also to Brentwood, Chelmsford and Harlow
Accommodation	Green Man (TL 515 024, on stage, Tel 01992 522255)

It doesn't take long to leave Epping behind. Soon you'll be treading the first green lane of the Essex Way, passing (or perhaps not) two of its first rural pubs, and experiencing wood and coppice, open fields and distant views – in short, a mix of all the things that characterise the route of the Way. Just short of Ongar, the church at Greensted is of international importance.

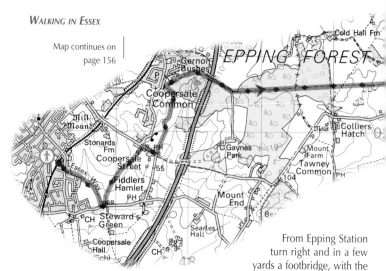

Map continues on
page 156

From Epping Station
turn right and in a few
yards a footbridge, with the
first Essex Way waymark (see the
Introduction for a picture), crosses the
railway. Over the tracks, walk down the cul-de-sac, turn
right at the road junction, and left at a concrete sign just
after Bower Court. The path crosses a field half-right on
a track and goes through a hedge gap. Turn left and at
a road turn left and then almost immediately left again,
onto a green lane that comes out to a road at **Coopersale
Street**. Turn right, passing the **Theydon Oak pub**, and
past Coopersale Lodge turn left at a concrete sign. Keep
on the left edge of fields, slowly uphill, to enter **Gernon
Bushes Nature Reserve** at a bench.

> The **reserve** has two distinct habitats, old gravel
> ponds now developing into bog in the north, and
> in the south the uppermost part of the Roding-
> tributary stream valley you have been ascending
> to reach it. The Essex Way, roughly, keeps to the
> boundary between them.

In the reserve turn left, across two boardwalks and up
steps to an information sign where you turn right. Some
200 metres further on, the Way leaves the reserve briefly

to follow the boundary of a cricket pitch. Back in the reserve, turn right after a boardwalk onto a bridleway, and cross the **M11** on a footbridge. There is extensive sweet chestnut coppicing after the motorway, followed by birch plantations. The bridleway becomes more straggly after these, but keeps a straight course out into arable land to follow an oak avenue.

Eventually, the bridleway reaches a water tower on higher ground ahead on your left, but you do not go there – instead look for a wooden marker about 250 metres before the tower, and take the path on your right. Cross a field to a gap at a marker and keep to the left edge of the field beyond before crossing a meadow. A gate in an electric fence leads out to **Toot Hill**.

At the road the Essex Way turns left, passing the **Green Man** pub, going through the village, and then turning right onto a path at a wooden sign by Weald Lodge. Turn immediately right, then in 50 metres cross a footbridge, and follow waymarks for over a kilometre. Turn left through a kissing gate, go through paddocks,

On the way to Toot Hill

and cross a minor road onto another path. At a metalled track turn right for St Andrew's church at **Greensted**.

St Andrew's is the first in a chain of remarkable churches that are passed on the Way, and sets the standard high: this is nothing less than the oldest surviving wooden church on earth. This results from the timber framing of the nave, dated to 1053; beneath the chancel are remains of an earlier chapel, from around the time of the missionary work of St Cedd. The wooden tower dates from the 1600s, and the capping oak spire from merely 2005! By the church entrance is a 12th-century Crusader grave.

When in 1837 the Tolpuddle martyrs (early trade unionists from Dorset) returned from transportation to Australia, they were resettled in this parish and in High Laver. The church register records the marriage in 1839 of one of them, James Brine, to his comrade's daughter Elizabeth Standfield.

Just beyond the church, turn left on the drive to **Greensted Hall**, and go ahead through a fence gap after **Church Lodge**. The path now heads directly to Ongar. As you near Ongar, you can see the track of the preserved Epping Ongar railway on your left. Cross the Roding tributary of Cripsey Brook and ascend to Budworth Hall on the High Street at Ongar. The rarely used 'Chipping' in the town's official title denotes a market town.

STAGE 3
Ongar to Salt's Green

Start	Budworth Hall, Ongar (TL 552 031)
Finish	Salt's Green, bus stops and parking area on the A1060 (TL 621 109)
Distance	8½ miles (13km)
Walking time	3½hr
Maps	OS Explorer 183, Landranger 167
Refreshments	In Ongar; Forrester's Arms in High Ongar, but otherwise none on route unless a diversion to the Queen's Head at Fyfield (adds ¾ mile/1km)
Public transport	Buses to Salt's Green from Chelmsford and Harlow
Accommodation	Mulberry House (TL 561 039, 200m from stage, Tel 01277 365398, www.mulberry-house.com), Diggins Farm (TL 581 082, 1.4km from stage, Tel 01277 899303)

This stage takes you past the site of Ongar's Norman castle to a quiet mile beside one of Essex's major rivers – never much more than a stream – the Roding, a Thames tributary which drains much of the county between the Lea on the western boundary and the North Sea rivers. Thereafter, the Way hurries on by way of two green lanes, always a haven from the sun and wind (but sometimes damp underfoot). In between is the unique, for Essex at least, double-churchyard at Willingale.

Cross the zebra crossing at Budworth Hall and walk past the King's Head Inn to the town sign. Here turn left past the **church** and continue on the path immediately to the right of the White House. Turn left through a kissing gate at a concrete sign. At a path junction in 220 metres, turn half-left; the Way keeps to the grass path, skirting a play area. Turn right at houses and left at the next path junction (not the path leading to a footbridge); when you meet the **A414**, turn right in the field rather than walking along the road until you can take steps up to the road and cross it.

Map continues on
page 160

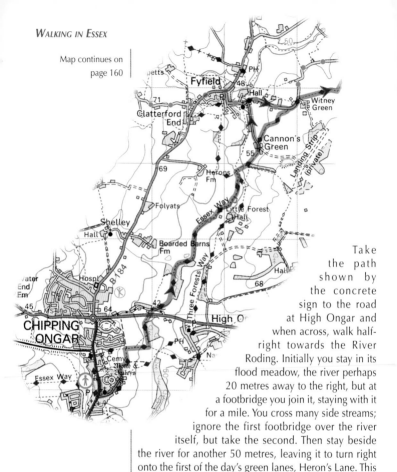

Take
the path
shown by
the concrete
sign to the road
at High Ongar and
when across, walk half-
right towards the River
Roding. Initially you stay in its
flood meadow, the river perhaps
20 metres away to the right, but at
a footbridge you join it, staying with it
for a mile. You cross many side streams;
ignore the first footbridge over the river
itself, but take the second. Then stay beside
the river for another 50 metres, leaving it to turn right
onto the first of the day's green lanes, Heron's Lane. This
comes out to a minor road at **Cannon's Green**, which
you follow for 100 metres, then turning right onto the
continuation of Heron's Lane. ◄

Heron's Lane comes out to a road, onto which you
turn right for 200 metres; this is the road you will have
taken if you have short-cut the diversion to Fyfield. Leave
it at the gate to 'Witney Green', across grass to a gate,
and cross a large field to a road. Turn left on the road, and
then right at a wooden sign just past a road junction. On

For food and drink,
continue on the road
past Fyfield church
to the Queen's Head.
Return either to here
or, having passed
the church, continue
ahead on the
Willingale road.

158

A TALE OF TWO CHURCHES

Today, the scattering of houses that makes up the settlement of Willingale may seem not to merit the building of two churches, but it was not always so. The first, and smaller, St Andrew's, has Norman origins; the second, St Christopher's, was built in response to the population increase which followed the 14th-century flourishing of the wool trade. A local legend holds that the second church was built by a wealthy local woman who so disliked her sister she built her own church rather than sit beside her on Sundays.

Each church, of course, had its own parish, Willingale Spain and Willingale Doe respectively, anglicisations of Norman families d'Epaigne and d'Eu; there is still a Spains Hall a mile south-east of the churches. The two parishes continued to amalgamation in 1929. St Andrew's had a wartime flourish when used as the chapel for American airmen based at the airfield just south of the village, but is now no longer used for regular services. It remains the more untouched of the two churches, St Christopher's having been heavily restored.

159

the path, look out for a right turn across a field, go over the footbridge, and take the clear field-side path to the larger of the two churches at Willingale.

Take the path on the right-hand side of Bell House (to 1988, the Bell Inn) opposite the churches. After the cricket field this keeps to the left of a hedgerow and then switches to the right in about 200 metres. Turn left over a footbridge, reaching a minor road in about half a mile. Go ahead onto a green lane with a compacted surface, and follow it for two miles to the hamlet of Pepper's Green; there's a quarter-mile where it joins the lane to Rowe's Farm, but a 'private property' sign makes it clear where to leave this stretch. From the hamlet, take the metalled road to the A1060 at the complementarily-named Salt's Green, where there is parking and bus stops.

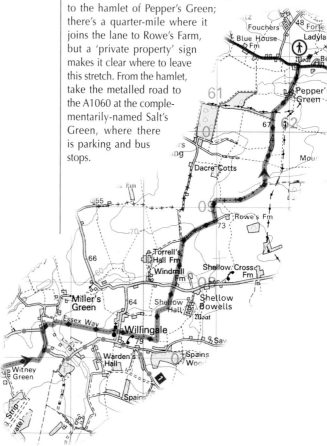

STAGE 4
Salt's Green to Great Waltham

Start	Salt's Green (TL 621 109)
Finish	Great Waltham, north end of village (TL 695 136)
Distance	8 miles (13km)
Walking time	3½hr
Maps	OS Explorer 183, Landranger 167
Refreshments	Leather Bottle pub in Pleshey; Beehive at Great Waltham, just off route
Public transport	Great Waltham has buses to Chelmsford and Stansted Airport
Accommodation	Acreland Green (TL 642 148, 300m from stage, Tel 01245 231277), Oakwrights Hall (TL 768 153, 200m from stage, Tel 01245 233 130, www.oakwrightshall.co.uk)

This walk continues the Stage 3 theme of using green lanes to travel deep through the Essex countryside, here to the historic village of Pleshey. This is the first stage of the Way, and its Epping Forest prelude, away from the influence of Thames-bound rivers; here you have passed over into the catchment of the Chelmer and its tributary the Can.

Good Easter

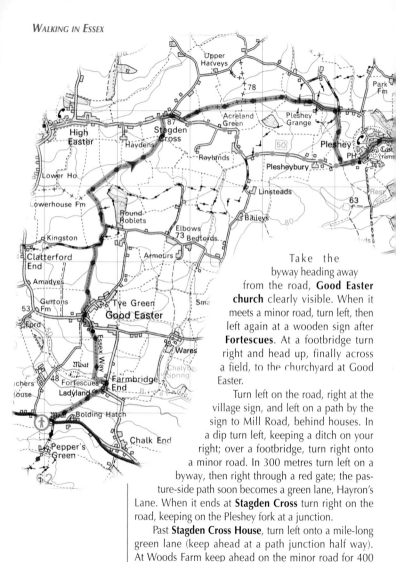

Take the byway heading away from the road, **Good Easter church** clearly visible. When it meets a minor road, turn left, then left again at a wooden sign after **Fortescues**. At a footbridge turn right and head up, finally across a field, to the churchyard at Good Easter.

Turn left on the road, right at the village sign, and left on a path by the sign to Mill Road, behind houses. In a dip turn left, keeping a ditch on your right; over a footbridge, turn right onto a minor road. In 300 metres turn left on a byway, then right through a red gate; the pasture-side path soon becomes a green lane, Hayron's Lane. When it ends at **Stagden Cross** turn right on the road, keeping on the Pleshey fork at a junction.

Past **Stagden Cross House**, turn left onto a mile-long green lane (keep ahead at a path junction half way). At Woods Farm keep ahead on the minor road for 400 metres, then turn right at a wooden sign onto the last green lane of the stage. Where it ends, turn left on the road into **Pleshey**, passing its church and pub, the excellent Leather Bottle. There is a pleasant green by the remnants of the castle moat just before the pub.

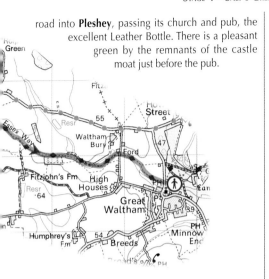

PLESHEY

To this day, the village of Pleshey sits within the 40 acres enclosed by the outer rampart and ditch of the Norman motte and bailey castle. Footpaths encircle many of the earthworks – the motte is up to 15m high – and viewing of the castle can be arranged by appointment.

In the reign of Richard II, the castle was owned by the Duke of Gloucester, very much a thorn in the king's side: as a 'Lord Appellant', he had trammelled the King's power and secured prosecution of his unpopular favourites. By 1388, Richard was king in name only.

This success did not last, and Richard did not forgive. In 1397 Richard visited Gloucester at Pleshey, apparently in friendship, but only to have him sent to Calais, later to be murdered. In *Richard II*, Shakespeare has his widow talk of the castle's subsequent decay to 'empty lodgings and unfurnished walls/Unpeopled offices, untrodden stones'

Within two years, Richard had been deposed by Henry IV. Another Henry – VIII – seized the castle at the time of the Dissolution, and its new owner John Gates found other uses for its stone.

Walking out of the village, look out for a small water-works on the right. Two paths leave here; you need the one that keeps the works fence on your right and joins the tiny Chelmer tributary of the Walthambury Brook, keeping it close for the rest of the stage. Just over 400 metres from the waterworks the path switches sides of the brook at an earth bridge, and about a kilometre further on, runs up to the bank of a reservoir; at the bank, turn right to follow the left edge of two fields, then turn right at a wooden marker. Across a road, the path continues to the bus stop at the most northerly houses in **Great Waltham**. ◄

For the Beehive pub, go down the road; the village shop is along Barrack Lane.

STAGE 5
Great Waltham to White Notley

Start	Great Waltham, north end of village (TL 695 136); parking at the village hall on South Street, TL 695 133
Finish	White Notley, Station Road (TL 787 184); parking in the village
Distance	11 miles (18km)
Walking time	5hr
Maps	OS Explorer 183, Landranger 167
Refreshments	Beehive at Great Waltham, just off route; Windmill at Chatham Green; Square and Compasses at Fuller Street; Owls Hill tea room at Terling; Cross Keys at White Notley
Public transport	White Notley station
Accommodation	None

For a relatively level county, Essex requires a lot of rivers to drain it. This stage crosses three of them, the Chelmer, Ter and Brain, each with its own personality; the smallest of them, the Ter, is close at hand for nearly half the stage, and a charming companion it is.

From the Crowbush House bus stop, go through the kissing gate. Over to your right across the park is the great

Queen Anne-period house of **Langleys**, designed by William Tufnell, but you do not go there yet. Instead take the grass path beside a three-tree copse, cross the first drive by two kissing gates, and turn right onto the second. On the path beside the house, there is a little dog graveyard; keep left here, and cross two bridges. After the second (which crosses the Chelmer) turn half-left and go through a kissing gate.

Keep ahead on this path over two roads – the second is the quite busy **B1008** – to a minor road in the hamlet of **Chatham Green**; turn left on this (unless you want the Windmill pub, to the right) and see how a small Essex settlement can give ribbon development a good name. At a road junction, go ahead on a concrete track, and just after a dip, turn half-right to cross a meadow. At the end of a field turn left, and soon right, to head for St John the Evangelist church at **Little Leighs**.

Map continues on page 166

Past the church, turn right, then right again. After the last house the road becomes a metalled path: keep ahead when it forks, so that you go under the busy A131 (the Ter beside you) rather than over. Cross the next road to a stile and go down the steps, back to the river.

In a short while, at a wooden sign just after a substantial bridge, the path turns left, away from the river, but only for 100 metres before turning right to keep above the river and parallel to it. Look for a stile in a barbed-wire fence and cross it, leading to a minor road (many people ignore the stile and continue lower down, off the right-of-way – but then a gate has to be climbed). Turn right onto the road and then, a little downhill, turn left up steps; at the next minor road, reached after a particularly attractive but alas boggy meadow, the path goes nearly straight over, but do look out for the natural spring here.

The Way now rises on a grass strip between fields, and then drops down into the hamlet of **Fuller Street**. The Square and Compasses pub, which still serves beer from the wood, and an Essex Way-dedicated phone box, are just to the left. The Way though takes the Terling road to just after Rose Cottage, where turn right (soon switching sides of the hedgerow) back down to and over the Ter. After this keep **Sandy Wood** on your left until, at a corner shown by a wooden marker by an oak tree, you take a cross-field path and then a lane into the straggly village of **Terling**.

Map continues on page 168

The seat of the **Lords Rayleigh** is at Terling Place, just to the south of the village. The third Baron Rayleigh, John Strutt, was a noted physicist

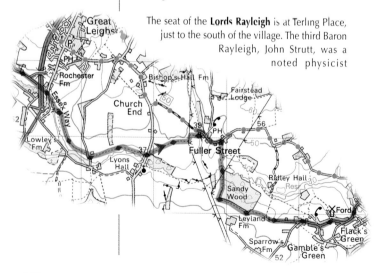

THE CRICKET BAT WILLOW

A mile from the River Ter is Wright's timberyard, home to the principal suppliers of cricket bat willow to batsmen and women the world over. They purchase, fell and re-plant stands of *Salix Alba Caerulea*, and supply it to makers both here and overseas.

Caerulea is the one variant of the willow family that can produce blades both strong and flexible enough to withstand repeated 90mph bombardment. It grows in other cricketing nations but needs English rain for the best quality. It thrives beside the streams and rivers that drain the heavy clay soils of Essex, and the walks in this guide pass many of the trees that they will use.

It is thought that *Caerulea* is a hybrid of the white willow and the crack willow, also both common in the county. They are not always easy to tell apart. The leaves of the white willow have a silky surface that reflects a white sheen in the light; those of the cricket-bat willow are more bluey-green and slightly larger. Crack willow is so-called owing to the propensity of branches to break off readily if struck at their base.

and winner of the 1904 Nobel prize. His work in acoustics still underpins the subject today; and, with Sir William Ramsay, he was the first to isolate the gas argon.

Essex Way information box, Fuller Street

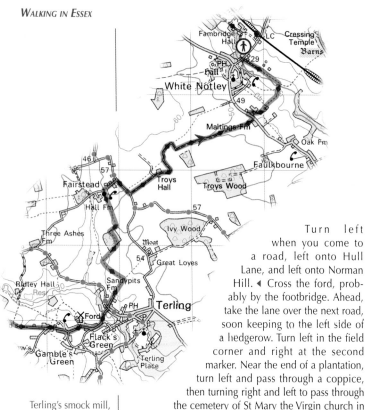

Turn left when you come to a road, left onto Hull Lane, and left onto Norman Hill. ◄ Cross the ford, probably by the footbridge. Ahead, take the lane over the next road, soon keeping to the left side of a hedgerow. Turn left in the field corner and right at the second marker. Near the end of a plantation, turn left and pass through a coppice, then turning right and left to pass through the cemetery of St Mary the Virgin church in the tiny hamlet of **Fairstead**.

Terling's smock mill, to the left just before Norman Hill, is owned by a former member of dance band The Prodigy.

If you only go into one Essex church while following this guide, make it **St Mary the Virgin**: it balances serenity from the unusual green of the stained glass with surprise from the 13th-century wall decoration. Outside, much Roman brick and tile has been reused in the making of the church.

Turn right on the minor road, right again, then left on a lane (not an earlier footpath). This becomes a green lane after **Troys Hall**. Where it ends, turn right through

a metal gate, then left on a concrete track. Cross a road and turn left, then right after Forge Cottage, later keeping to the left of a house. Ahead is the third of the stage's three rivers, the Brain. Cross it on a footbridge and turn left, staying close to it to a road. Turn left for the village of **White Notley** and its pub the **Cross Keys**. Turn right to continue the Way (for 50 metres, then left) or for the station.

Approaching the River Brain

Diversion
The spectacular 13th-century Cressing Temple Barns, built for the Knights Templar, are a kilometre from the footbridge over the Brain. To reach them, turn right instead of left, then left in 100 metres. Cross the railway and go straight across the field from the kissing gate.

STAGE 6
White Notley to Coggeshall

Start	White Notley, Station Road (TL 787 184; park in the village)
Finish	Coggeshall church (TL 853 229)
Distance	7½ miles (12km)
Walking time	3½hr
Maps	OS Explorer 183/195, Landranger 167/168
Refreshments	Cross Keys at White Notley; pubs and cafés in Coggeshall
Public transport	Buses at Coggeshall to Chelmsford, Braintree, Marks Tey and Colchester
Accommodation	White Hart (TL 849 225, 350m from stage, Tel 01376 561654)

This stage heads past the church at Cressing, with its links to the medieval Knights Templar, towards the Blackwater Valley, well seen from the approach into Coggeshall. This is one of the areas of Essex where the Kesgrave sands cover the clay soil, and sand and gravel extraction continue to this day. The highlight is undoubtedly Coggeshall itself; the Way only skirts the town, which is far too good to miss – see the notes at the end for a quick tour, or come back another day.

From White Notley village, walk towards the station; from the station platform, turn right. The Essex Way takes a lane to **Fambridge Hall** just north of the ford over the River Brain – don't worry about the 'private road' sign. Past the hall turn left, and soon right to go under the railway. When you come to a road, cross it and turn left, then go right at a concrete sign on a path that leads to All Saints church at **Cressing**.

The Way takes the path running to the right of the churchyard. Keep the buildings of **Egypts Farm** on your left (except for a couple of new barns), turn right on the road for 250 metres, and take the path on the left. The next stretch is quite complex, with a succession of turns

Abbey Lane,
Coggeshall

every 300 to 400 metres. There's a right turn just before a wood, then a left turn (no marker – look for a marker post across the field, between pylons)) to cross a field. Next turn right onto the headland, go through a gap, and at the next gap turn left (marker). In a dip, turn right, with a ditch beside you on your left – an important turn, but again there is no marker here.

You come to and cross both a minor road and a works road leading to a sandpit. Turn right on the next minor road, then left where it turns right. Ahead of you is the **River Blackwater**, which you will view from the southern slopes of its valley all the way to Coggeshall. At first, Bradwell Farm is beside you, with its rather untraditional crops of trout and alpaca. After a gravel pit the Way turns right, up towards **Curd Hall Farm**; when level with the farm, turn left on a track which leads to Grange Barn, another of the great grain barns of the county (see Walk 15).

Derelict after 20 years of neglect in 1982, Grange Barn was purchased by Braintree Council in the nick of time, and restored to its present glory. It is now cared for by the National Trust.

Go ahead on the gravelled Abbey

Lane. This passes the **chapel of St Nicholas**, formerly the gatehouse of an abbey (owners of the barn) founded in 1120, and just before the Blackwater, the abbey's Abbot's Lodging. Look for the stone by the chapel noting the half-way point of the Way. Some 80 metres after crossing the river turn left, and when you meet the east-west road through Coggeshall – this is the route of the Roman Stane Street – turn left again. At a playing field, go through a gate, keeping to the right side of the field to come out to **Coggeshall church**.

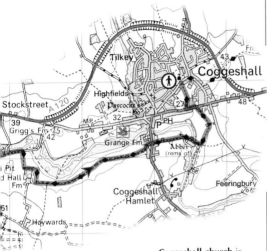

Coggeshall church is dedicated to St Peter ad Vincula – the same dedicatee as the Saxon chapel at Bradwell-on-Sea – and is one of the great woollen churches of eastern England, testimony of the medieval wealth of the wool trade.

A LOOP THROUGH COGGESHALL

The creators of the Essex Way had a dilemma: go past the abbey or through the historic centre of Coggeshall? The Way could not do both. But you can do both with this little two-mile loop. Although it has nothing like the name recognition of the more famous Dedham or Thaxted, Coggeshall is easily the architectural equal of both.

From the church, walk past the Woolpack Inn down Church Street past a succession of listed buildings – around forty in all. Many of the frontages hide even older buildings; for example, the plaque on Spooners shows

1467, but parts of the house itself are a century older. Prominent at the junction with Stoneham Street is the late 18th-century clock tower. Past the White Horse Hotel, continue onto West Street for Paycocke's, full of glorious carving inside and out, flaunting the wool-trade wealth of its eponymous owner when built in 1500. Conrad Noel, later benefactor of Gustav Holst (see Walk 20), lived here before moving to Thaxted.

Back-track now. If you are continuing on the Essex Way, continue along East Street to the playing field and hence church rather than return by Church Street. For a stand-alone walk, however, turn right onto The Gravel, right onto Bridge Street, and go up to the Abbey Barn; then continue to the church by the Essex Way.

As well as its architectural heritage, Coggeshall has several claims to manufacturing fame. Brick-making returned to England here in the 12th century; although the wool trade declined in the 16th century, cloth, silk, velvet and lace followed it; and the town was the brewing capital of Essex in Victorian times, as can be seen from the several surviving brewery chimneys. Its adjuncts, gelatine and isinglass, were made here to the 1980s.

STAGE 7
Coggeshall to Fordstreet Bridge

Start	Coggeshall church (TL 853 229)
Finish	Fordstreet Bridge (TL 920 271); or for a train station finish use Chappell & Wakes Colne station
Distance	6½ miles (11km)
Walking time	3hr
Maps	OS Explorer 195/184, Landranger 168
Refreshments	Pubs and cafés in Coggeshall; Chequers at Great Tey; café and Shoulder of Mutton pub in Fordstreet
Public transport	Buses at Fordstreet to Halstead and Colchester; or trains from Chappell & Wakes Colne station, 6½ miles from Coggeshall, 2½ miles from Fordstreet
Accommodation	King's Arms (TL 878 231, 400m from stage, Tel 01376 562006, www.kingsarmsbandb.co.uk), Rosebank (TL 897 288, on alternative route, Tel 01787 223552)

There's a bit of Essex tableland walking to start with, along the flat headlands and fields north of Stane Street, but from Great Tey it is not far to the pretty Colne Valley – a good place to practice willow-tree spotting, using the hints in Stage 5.

From Coggeshall church, walk away from the **Woolpack**, and turn right onto St Peter's Road. Take the path on the left opposite St Anne's Close, and cross the Coggeshall bypass with care. Beyond, you have a ditch on your left at first, but look out for the switch of sides down steps and over a footbridge. At a minor road, do a quick right/left turn onto a wide track. When it veers left, you go ahead, onto a wide headland. The Way twice switches sides of a headrow and comes out to a minor road at **East Gores**. Turn right here, and left after 'Whytegates'.

Go past the end of a narrow fir copse and keep ahead, staying on the left side of a large field. Cross two

175

Autumn fields beyond East Gores

footbridges, turning right after the second, then keep a wood on your right. After the wood ends, cross 50 metres of field to a footbridge (despite what the waymarker

Map continues on page 178

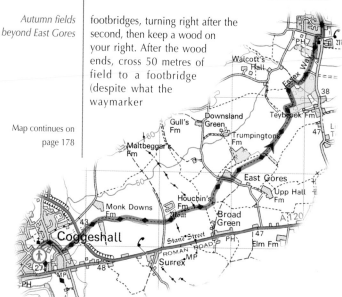

shows), and keep ahead. Later veer right to avoid a concrete track and you will come out to the church and Chequers pub at **Great Tey**. ▶

The pub has a double function, also housing the village shop.

> To your right is **St Barnabas church**, castle-like in its bulk. Yet once it was even larger – the entire west end was demolished in 1829, as too unsafe and expensive to repair; the demolition bill came to be twice the repair estimate. The red brick is Roman.

Turn right at the pub, then left onto Chappel Road. Look out for a right turn at 'Bellevue House' – the sign may be obscured, and the Way is pinched in by the showy balustrades of its carpark. At the end of a field, turn left, and in a while the path is a green lane – note the half-right turn at the path junction with farm buildings beyond, and another soon after. Now, views across the Colne Valley open up; the river will be your companion for the next four miles, in this stage and the next. At 'Applecroft', take the lane half-right over the railway, and continue through **Bacon's Farm**, perhaps setting geese cackling. Turn left through a

The pub garden at Great Tey

gate opposite an old barn, and walk down the left side of the field to the river.

Alternative rail route

Chappel & Wakes Colne station is only just over a mile from here. To reach it, go left through the gate by the pillbox, cross a field either side of Pope's Hall, then follow the path by the viaduct, crossing underneath it at arch 14. Over a footbridge, turn left on the main road,

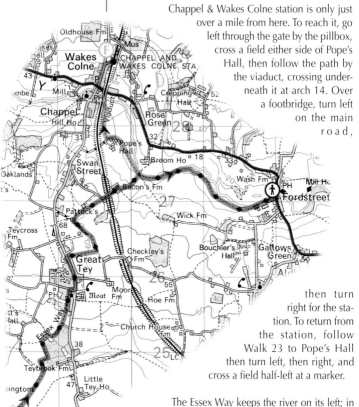

then turn right for the station. To return from the station, follow Walk 23 to Pope's Hall then turn left, then right, and cross a field half-left at a marker.

The Essex Way keeps the river on its left; in about half a mile a willow plantation will keep you away from the river for a while, but the path is clear all the way to **Fordstreet**. Just before you get there, Millrace garden centre has a café. This stage of the Way turns left to finish at Fordstreet Bridge, over the Colne.

STAGE 8

Fordstreet Bridge to Great Horkesley

Start	Fordstreet Bridge (TL 920 271)
Finish	Half Butt Inn, Great Horkesley (TL 981 292)
Distance	5 miles (8km)
Walking time	2½hr
Maps	OS Explorer 184, Landranger 168
Refreshments	café and Shoulder of Mutton pub in Fordstreet; three pubs in West Bergholt, off route; Half Butt Inn at Great Horkesley
Public transport	buses from Great Horkesley to Sudbury and Colchester (not Sundays)
Accommodation	None

The tranquil Colne is followed closely for the first part of this stage, much of it within the Woodland Trust's Fordham Hall Estate. After the sprawling village of West Bergholt, a few little ups and downs bring the stage to a close.

From the north end of the bridge, go through the garden of the Shoulder of Mutton to join the River Colne, then entering the Fordham Hall Estate. At a telegraph pole, there's a left turn to avoid a river meander, but the estate's brightly patterned marker posts will keep you on track through the estate's domain. Cross a road, turn left

Map continues on page 181

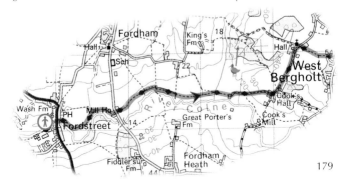

Colne Valley meadows

onto a grass path, then go through willows, into the river's flood meadows.

The **Fordham Hall Estate** was donated to the Woodland Trust in 2002. More than half of its 200ha, mostly encircling the village of Fordham to the north, has already been stocked with nearly 50,000 trees. The remainder, mostly the Essex Way stretch by the Colne, has been resown with grass and wild flowers for grazing and hay-cutting; already, wetland plants such as purple loosestrife, brooklime and flag iris are colonising the damper patches of the flood meadows. There are otters in the river and barn owls and skylarks in the skies; for the walker, the Trust has added 10km of permissive paths to the 10km of rights-of-way that already existed.

Waymarker on the Fordham Hall Estate

At a derelict brick barn, go through a gate and along the lane, leaving the Colne. The lane veers left through a farm, keeping cottage number 2 to your right. Near the top of the hill, keep a hedgerow to your left, before you go through a gap in front of the hall and church at **West Bergholt**.

> The north wall of **West Bergholt church** is Saxon, and it is possible that one of the timbers in the belfry was originally used in a wooden west wall – if so, that places the church on a par with Greensted (Stage 2). The church is no longer used, as by the end of Victorian times the bulk of houses no longer surrounded the manor house and church but the present site to the south-east; parishioners were reluctant to make the journey, and a new church was opened in the village in 1904.

Look for the wooden sign directing the Way along the left side of a field. At a junction, veer half-left to the nearest houses. In the village proper follow the sign to the new parish church. After this, turn left at shops, right at the village sign, and left into Armoury Road. ▶ Follow this as it veers right out of the village. Turn left at **Armoury Farm** and veer very slightly right with a ditch on your right to a marker, where you turn left to cross a field. In a dip, keep ahead on another cross-field path. Taking a slight left turn

There are three village pubs. For the Queen's Head, turn right at the shops; for the Treble Tile and White Hart, turn left at the village sign.

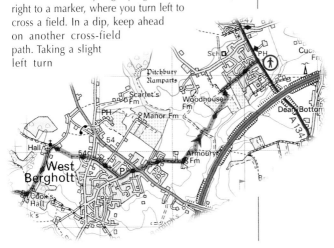

THE SITING OF ESSEX CHURCHES

Hall, barn and church at West Bergholt

The move of West Bergholt church to its people has not happened in many other sites across the county. Many of the churches in this book – including those at Lambourne (Walk 9), Matching (Walk 12), Debden (Walk 15), Chrishall (Walk 16), Ashdon (Walk 18), and on the Essex Way at Cressing, Boxted, Langham and Lawford – are all now some distance from the principal settlement of that name, although they are usually right next to the manor house.

The historian Norman Scarfe showed that 'an Essex parish tended to identify with its dominant manor', maybe taking the name of its usually Norman lord, in a way that almost never happened even in adjoining Suffolk. No doubt those twin seats of local medieval power, the lord and the priest, gained much by their mutual proximity; but for the villagers more practical considerations will have held sway as they carved out homesteads from the native forest, even if a weekly trek to the church became more awkward as a result.

through a gap, head for a black weatherboarded house. Walk past this down a lane into **Great Horkesley**; the Half Butt Inn is just to your left.

STAGE 9
Great Horkesley to Dedham

Start	Half Butt Inn, Great Horkesley (TL 981 292)
Finish	Dedham church (TM 057 331); parking on Mill Road (TM 057 333)
Distance	9 miles (15km)
Walking time	4hr
Maps	OS Explorer 196, Landranger 168
Refreshments	Half Butt Inn at Great Horkesley; Sun Inn, Marlborough Head and tea shops in Dedham
Public transport	Buses from Dedham to Colchester, also (Sundays only) Harwich
Accommodation	Sun Inn (TM 057 031, on route, Tel 01206 323351, www.thesuninndedham.com), Dedham Hall (TM 059 332, 100m from stage, Tel 01206 323027, www.dedhamhall. co.uk)

The influence of the Stour is strong throughout this stage. Boxted sits on a little ridge and affords the first glimpses; beyond Rivers Hall, the river is in clear view through a long descent before the sharp rise up to one of Constable's most-painted buildings, Langham church. The Stour's banks are not far from here, and soon you are in one of England's loveliest lowland landscapes, Dedham Vale.

With the **Half Butt Inn** on your left, walk along the main road. Turn right onto Ivy Lodge Road and then, after 'Saxon House', left at a concrete sign onto a path which becomes a concrete track after houses. Where this splits, take the right turn, and then look out for a quarter-left turn across a field, leading into a wood. (If the field is in crop, stay on the track and turn left at the wood edge to enter the wood at a marker.) The woodland path comes out at a building. Turn left on a road and right onto the next road, following this for half a mile to **Holly Lodge Farm**. Turn right on a concrete track to go past a black barn and

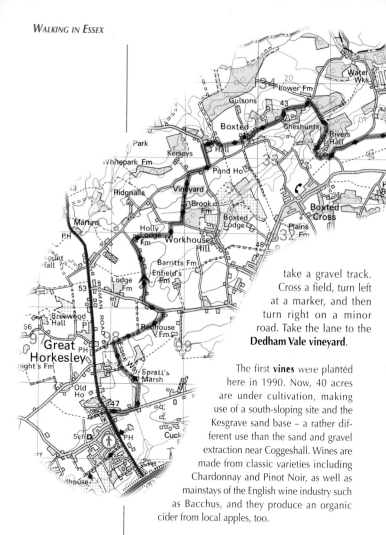

take a gravel track. Cross a field, turn left at a marker, and then turn right on a minor road. Take the lane to the **Dedham Vale vineyard**.

The first **vines** were planted here in 1990. Now, 40 acres are under cultivation, making use of a south-sloping site and the Kesgrave sand base – a rather different use than the sand and gravel extraction near Coggeshall. Wines are made from classic varieties including Chardonnay and Pinot Noir, as well as mainstays of the English wine industry such as Bacchus, and they produce an organic cider from local apples, too.

Continue on a green lane with the vineyard on your right. Beyond the vineyard, look out for a gap on your right, where you cross a footbridge and swap sides of the hedgerow. Turn right on a minor road, then left (signposted

Nayland), leaving this road to turn right through Boxted Hall Farm. Veer right in the farmyard, then turn left at Little Church House to follow a path to St Peter's Church at **Boxted**.

Go through the churchyard, the church on your left, and turn left onto a minor road. After the last houses, the

Dedham Vale vineyard

first sight of the Stour Valley, and the Essex border, is over to your left. Leave the road for a track on your right, just before reaching a thatched barn. The Way makes its way cautiously around the Georgian mansion of Rivers Hall. At the top of the hill, with the house just beyond the 'private' signs, look for a concrete sign. Turn half-right here, keep a large corrugated shed on your left, and past the little black-painted estate office, turn left at another concrete sign. Stay on the field edge. At a gate, you will find yourself looking at a lime tree sitting in the middle of a little grass triangle.

From here do not take the minor road which leads directly away from Rivers Hall but the one across the triangle. Leave the road at a stile by a concrete sign on your right, crossing the field to a marker at the right edge of a small wood. Join a gravel track at a gap after a house, do a quick left/right turn over a minor road, and continue across fields to a lodge on another minor road. Here take the metalled lane for about 300 metres to a gate, and cross to the next gate. In the meadow after a wood, look for a glimpse of St Mary's church at Langham up above you; soon, at a marker, you turn sharp right to reach it.

At both **Boxted and Langham churches** important new work has been undertaken. At Boxted, the chancel ceiling is decorated in a striking night-time blue, commemorating the Hale-Bopp comet seen in 1998 and the total eclipse of the sun of 1999. Langham has a new organ, built by Roger Pulham between 1997 and 2004, and a new wooden gallery.

This is an alternative break point, with a better weekday bus service than Dedham. The stop is just over half a kilometre north, at the Black Horse pub.

Some 80 metres beyond the church, take the left-hand of two lime tree avenues. Eventually you come to a road, once the A12. ◄ Turn left on this, then right on the Dedham road, over the new **A12**. Turn left to the elegant hotel of Milsoms. Just in front of its car park, turn sharp right at a concrete sign into woods. At a gate, you come to the banks of the Stour; immediately you see why a painter might have flourished here. Follow waymarkers for both the Way and FP2, through the Stour's flood meadows at first, then through a kissing gate for field-boundaries to Bridges Farm, and finally out onto the High Street at **Dedham**.

STAGE 10
Dedham to Wrabness

Start	Dedham war memorial (TM 057 331); free parking on Mill Lane (TM 057 334)
Finish	Wrabness church (TM 174 318)
Distance	10 miles (16km); can be split into two equal sections using Mistley station
Walking time	4½hr
Maps	OS Explorer 196/197, Landranger 168
Refreshments	Pubs and cafés in Manningtree; Thorn hotel and café at Mistley; Stranger's Home pub in Bradfield
Public transport	Wrabness station
Accommodation	Emsworth House (TM 140 312, 500m from stage, Tel 01255 870860, www.emsworthhouse.co.uk)

At first the walk heads uphill through paddocks and meadows, before skirting the housing of Lawford and dropping down to the estuarial Stour at historic Manningtree and Mistley. From here there are some interesting woods before Wrabness Nature Reserve, an important site for bird life especially in winter.

From Dedham war memorial, walk past the Duchy Barn and turn right behind the cricket pavilion. Before you reach the end of the boundary, turn left through a kissing gate. Just past a footbridge, turn half-left at a marker, and over another footbridge, walk up to and past the pink house ahead. Turn right on a minor road, then left on an (initially) gravel track just past 'Hunter's Moon'. The Way eventually crosses a meadow to turn right onto a road. Turn left onto Anchor Lane for 30 metres and then keep ahead to a minor road, where you turn right for 250 metres. Turn left through a gap with a kissing gate, cross half-right to a minor road, and go over, through paddocks to the main railway line. Cross this with care, making sure you can neither see nor hear any trains.

Go into a wood over a plank bridge. At 'Slumberlands' the Way follows a lane to 'Brown Knolls', where through a gate you turn right, and later right onto a road. Beside 'The Lodge', turn left through a wooden gate onto a gravel track. Go through a kissing gate on your right, heading to another; **St Mary the Virgin church** at Lawford is just beyond, although the Way does not enter its churchyard.

Turn left at a wooden sign by the Old School House. Soon for the first time there are estuary views – tidal Essex is being reached, very different territory to that which the Way has followed so far. Turn half-right into a dip, go through a ramshackle kissing gate, gain height, then beside a house join the lane running to the A137 at Cox's Hill. ◀

The pavement beside the road leads downhill to Manningtree station in about ten minutes.

Cross the road, turn left and opposite a bench turn right onto the path through Owl's Flight Dell. Reaching suburban **Lawford**, keep a marshy area on your right before taking a metalled path with a school on your

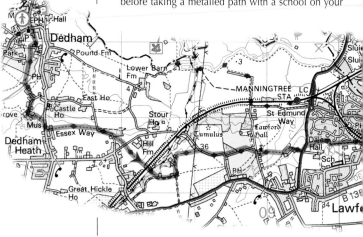

188

Lawford Church

right. Cross over a road and continue ahead, on a road that dips then climbs. Turn left over the railway onto Trinity Road, which soon becomes South Street – make sure you bear right to pass the Methodist church. You are now in **Manningtree** – rather remote from its railway station, like many an Essex village is from its church. Keep ahead over the High Street,

Map continues on page 190

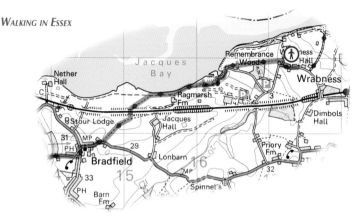

turning right by a builders' mer-chants, the Stour just over the yard.

Stay on the road along Mistley Walls, beside the river now, and Mistley Towers, the strange remnant of a Robert Adam church. The main landmark in Mistley itself is the maltings, and the Way goes straight through this sweetest-smelling of all industrial sites. ◄ **Mistley station** is just beyond the entrance to the maltings. Turn right at

The many swans here on the Stour thrive on waste from the maltings.

Poppies at Lawford

a concrete sign into the maltings, along the pedestrian route shown. At the end of the site, go through a metal gate in a wire fence, and in 20 metres turn left, up steps and under the railway.

Cross parkland on a faint track and go through a pair of kissing gates. Do not go through the next kissing gate, but turn left over an earth bridge, keeping ahead at a further kissing gate to rise through **Furze Hill Woods** – mostly oak and beech – an old fence your guide Beyond, continue to a road, turn right for a few yards, and then left through a kissing gate beside 'Wymarks'. This path crosses three fields until turning left to join a minor road into **Bradfield**.

The site was used for storing mines until 1963. Plans for a prison here were rejected; the site was finally saved from development in 1992.

Turn left in the village, passing the church. Opposite the pub, turn right onto Harwich Road for 300 metres, then turn left on a path. Go under the railway again, keep ahead to the estuary, then turn right and follow it until you enter **Wrabness Nature Reserve**. ▶ Turn left on an asphalt path and follow markers until a left fork is shown. Go down steps and turn left on a gravel path, leading to steps up to the sea wall, which you follow for just 150 metres until concrete steps lead down again. Go through a metal barrier onto a green lane; where it ends, turn right onto a concrete track then quickly left onto a minor road to All Saints Church at **Wrabness**. ▶ For Wrabness station, continue along the road, and turn left after the railway bridge.

The wooden building in the churchyard is a bell-cage, a temporary building more than 300 years old.

MATTHEW HOPKINS, WITCHFINDER-GENERAL

Matthew Hopkins exploited the religious superstitions of the 17th century to torture and have killed two hundred or so, mostly women, on grounds of their witchcraft. He did this within the space of three years, while in his mid-twenties, from his home in Manningtree. Essex loyalists can console themselves that Hopkins was Suffolk-born, of the rector of Great Wenham. He had some legal training, but not enough work to make the practice pay, or at least pay enough for his wants.

The previous king, James I, had considered himself something of an authority on 'daemonology' and caused a new, harsh law to be enacted. A strand in English Puritanism took this forward in the first Charles's reign, and it is this which Hopkins exploited.

His first case (March 1644) was conveniently close to home, 'seven or eight of that horrible sect of Witches living in the Towne where he lived', he later wrote (albeit not in the first person). The first he stripped naked to examine for the Devil's third teat, establishing a penchant for humiliation and torture (deliberately short of the crudest physical violence, specifically forbidden under separate law) that would serve him well.

Exploiting the febrile religious tensions of the Civil War, Hopkins encouraged neighbour to inform on neighbour, and soon had enough work in the county to establish a team of four investigators around him. This led to the Chelmsford trials of July 1645, and his first 29 hangings. He then took upon himself the 'Witchfinder-General' title, alleging a commission from Parliament when there was no such thing, and set about purging East Anglia and Essex of witches – for a fee, £1 a town plus lavish expenses.

There was opposition, and it was effective. People began to ask whether it took a Satanist to find a Satanist. After arranging a hanging roughly twice a week, Hopkins effectively retired from his trade early in 1647, and by August he was dead of TB. He is buried in Mistley churchyard.

STAGE 11
Wrabness to Harwich

Start	Wrabness church (TM 174 318)
Finish	Harwich lower lighthouse (TM 261 324); parking on Wellington Road (TM 261 327)
Distance	9 miles (14km)
Walking time	4hr
Maps	OS Explorer 197, Landranger 168
Refreshments	Castle Inn at Ramsey; beach cafés in Dovercourt; pubs and cafés in Harwich
Public transport	Harwich Town station, buses to Clacton and Colchester
Accommodation	Bottle Kiln (TM 256 315, 150m from stage, Tel 01255 388439, www.jdwetherspoon.com), Swanhouse (TM 259 327, 300m from stage, Tel 07376 645853)

For its last stretch, the Way switches over from estuary to coast – appropriately, for the sea has shaped the county in so many ways. And Harwich, with its maritime past and present, is as fine and natural a finish point as any a long-distance walk can boast.

With **Wrabness church** on your left, walk along the road, and turn left to Stone Lane caravan site. Turn right just before wooden chalets and join the sea wall. The path stays close to the estuary for over a mile, passing through a coppice and later (using two very tall kissing gates) the grounds of a house ▸ At the end of a meadow, turn right into the woodland of the Stour Estuary Nature Reserve, veering left at the first junction. Cross the railway bridge and continue on a track through Copperas Wood to a road. Turn left on the road for 350 metres, then right on a track at a wooden sign. Where this turns right, go ahead across a field to a kissing gate at a gap in the hedgerow and then turn left, aiming for the **Ramsey windmill** (the path keeps to its left). Reaching a road, turn left.

Veer right at the **Castle Inn** to a roundabout, crossing the **A120** at the Harwich sign. Pass the village hall

Up to the right, you can just see Grayson Perry's 'House for Essex' through the trees. To reach it, take the path signposted 'Wrabness Community Shop'.

Map continues on page 194

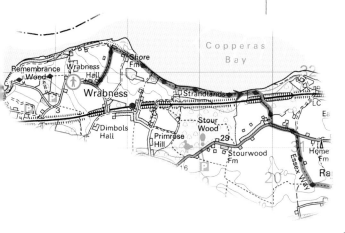

Dovercourt Bay at twilight

and opposite house number 5 turn right onto a hedged path, then turn left after a footbridge. Where the wood turns left at a marker, you keep ahead over a little rise. Just over 150 metres from a footbridge, turn left at a marker, pass a pavilion, and cross a road to a bridleway. Ahead now is the Naze Tower – linking the first walk in this book to the last. Where the gravel track turns right, you turn left, then right down steps. Continue to the sea wall and turn left onto it.

Follow the sea wall to the prom at **Dovercourt**. Pass the two cast-iron lighthouses, built in 1863 to replace the High and Low lighthouses you will soon come to. The port at Felixstowe has been in view for some time, but nevertheless the spectacle it presents at the turn by the breakwater is breath-taking – this, plus the Georgian (and earlier) distinction of the maritime heritage of Harwich, would be a worthy sight for the end of any long-distance walk.

Continue past the Low Lighthouse and the **treadmill crane**, turning left here for the (inland) High Lighthouse. A plaque here marks the end of the Essex Way. Well done! Congratulate yourself for a moment, then perhaps stroll up to the town quay or refresh yourself in a Harwich pub. The station is just over the road from the High Lighthouse, to help the journey home.

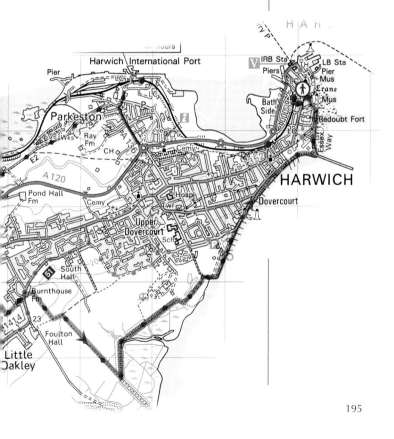

Harwich Maritime Museum

At Harwich, you have three options.
- Go home, and start planning your next long-distance walk.
- Take the little ferry (Easter to September) from Ha'Penny pier to Shotley or Felixstowe, and start walking on the Suffolk Coast Path. There is a Cicerone guide to help you.
- Take a much larger ferry from Parkeston Quay to Holland. The Essex Way from Manningtree to Ramsey is part of the Stranraer-to-Nice cross-European trail the E2.

The writer can't claim to have done the third, but that doesn't mean you can't go one better!

APPENDIX A

Route summary table

Walk	Start	Finish	Distance	Walking time	Page
1	Walton-on-the-Naze pier	Walton-on-the-Naze pier	5½ miles (9km)	2½hr	28
2	Cudmore Grove nature reserve, Mersea Island	Cudmore Grove nature reserve, Mersea Island	13½ miles (22km) or 5½ miles (9km)	5½ or 2½hr	32
3	Tollesbury	Tollesbury	17½ miles (29km) or 7 miles (11km)	7½ or 3 hours	38
4	Bradwell-on-Sea	Bradwell-on-Sea	10½ miles (17km) or 6½ miles (10km)	4½ or 3hr	44
5	Burnham-on-Sea or Althorne stations	North Fambridge station	10½ miles (17km) or 5½ miles (9km)	4½ or 2½hr	49
6	Leigh-on-Sea station	Leigh-on-Sea station	8 miles (13km)	3½hr	53
7	Orsett	Orsett	5 miles (8km)	2½hr	60
8	Bedford's Park, Havering-atte-Bower	Bedford's Park, Havering-atte-Bower	4½ miles (7km)	2hr	63
9	Hainault Forest Country Park	Hainault Forest Country Park	6 miles (10km)	3hr	66
10	Mill Green	Mill Green	5½ miles (9km)	2½hr	70
11	Danbury	Danbury	10 miles (16km)	4½hr	74

Walk	Start	Finish	Distance	Walking time	Page
12	Moreton	Moreton	10½ miles (17km)	4½hr	79
13	Roydon station	Harlow Mill station	7½ miles (12km) or 5½ miles (9km)	3½ or 2½hr	84
14	Takeley Street	Takeley Street	6 miles (10km)	3hr	89
15	Debden (by Saffron Walden) or Newport	Debden or Newport	6 miles (9km) or 7½ miles (11km)	2½hr or 3hr	93
16	Arkesden	Arkesden	11 miles (18 km)	5hr	97
17	Great Chesterford	Saffron Walden or Great Chesterford	13 miles (21 km) or 8½ miles (14 km)	5½ or 4hr	102
18	Ashdon	Ashdon	6 miles (10km)	3hr	109
19	Radwinter	Radwinter	5½ miles (9km)	2½hr	113
20	Thaxted	Thaxted	9 miles (14km)	4hr	117
21	Finchingfield	Finchingfield	5½ miles (9km)	2½hr	122
22	Castle Hedingham	Castle Hedingham	7 miles (11km)	3hr	125
23	Chappel & Wakes Colne station	Chappel & Wakes Colne station	8 miles (13km) or 4½ miles (7km)	3½ or 2hr	129
24	Bures station	Sudbury station	7½ miles (12km)	3½hr	135

Walk	Start	Finish	Distance	Walking time	Page
25	Manningtree station	Manningtree station	7 miles (11km)	3hr	139
Across Essex					
Stage 1	Manor Park station	Epping station	14½ miles (23km)	6hr	145
Stage 2	Epping station	Ongar	7½ miles (12km)	3½hr	153
Stage 3	Ongar	Salt's Green	8½ miles (13km)	3½hr	157
Stage 4	Salt's Green	Great Waltham	8 miles (13km)	3½hr	161
Stage 5	Great Waltham	White Notley	11 miles (18km)	5hr	164
Stage 6	White Notley	Coggeshall	7½ miles (12km)	3½hr	170
Stage 7	Coggeshall	Fordstreet Bridge	6½ miles (11km)	3hr	175
Stage 8	Fordstreet Bridge	Great Horkesley	5 miles (8km)	2½hr	179
Stage 9	Great Horkesley	Dedham	9 miles (15km)	4hr	183
Stage 10	Dedham	Wrabness	10 miles (16km)	4½hr	187
Stage 11	Wrabness	Harwich	9 miles (14km)	4hr	192
Total			**96½ miles (155km)**	**43hr**	

APPENDIX B
Useful contacts

Many websites give Essex walking routes, including essexpubwalks.com, essexwalker. org, essexwalks.com, walkinginessex.co.uk and wildessex.net.

Tourist Information Centres

Colchester
Hollytrees Museum
Castle Park, Colchester CO1 1UG
Tel 01206 282920

Maldon
Wenlock Way
High Street, Maldon CM9 5AD
Tel 01621 856503

Saffron Walden
1 Market Place
Market Square
Saffron Walden CB10 1HR
Tel 01799 524002

Southend-on-Sea
Southend Pier
Southend-on-Sea SS1 1EE
Tel 01702 618747

Witham
Town Hall
61 Newland Street
Witham CM8 2FE
Tel 01376 502674

Visit Essex
County Hall, Market Road
Chelmsford CM1 1QH
Tel 03330 130177
www.visitessex.com

Other useful contacts
Epping Forest Visitor Centre (closed
Mon–Wed except Bank Holidays)
Nursery Road
High Beach IG10 4AF
Tel 020 8508 0028

Essex County Council Rights of Way team
County Hall
Market Road
Chelmsford CM1 1QH
Tel 01245 437291
prow.web@essexcc.gov.uk
(For rights of way in Southend, Thurrock
or the London Boroughs, contact the
relevant council)

Essex Wildlife Trust
Abbotts Hall Farm
Great Wigborough CO5 7RZ
Tel 01621 862960
www.essexwt.org.uk

Hatfield Forest
Tel 01279 870678
Hedingham Castle
Tel 01787 460261
www.hedinghamcastle.co.uk

English Heritage
www.english-heritage.org.uk

National Trust
www.nationaltrust.org.uk

Royal Society for the Protection of Birds
www.rspb.org.uk

APPENDIX C
Nine more long-distance paths in Essex

Chipping Ongar (Across Essex, Stage 3)

If you've enjoyed following the Essex Way in this book, then the county has plenty more long-distance routes for you to try.

The Essex Way was just one of the routes laid down by Fred Matthews and Harry Bitten. Here are three others they described.

- The **Harcamlow Way**, as its name suggests, runs from Harlow to Cambridge – and then back again, in a figure-of-eight centred on Newport. The bulk of the walk is in the county but as well as Cambridgeshire, the Way visits Hertfordshire. Recently waymarked,

it's a substantial undertaking at 141 miles; a good challenge, to walk it in eight days from a Cambridge base, is described on the author's website at www.trailman.co.uk as the 'Cambridge Eight'.

- The 41 miles of **St Peter's Way** lead from Chipping Ongar to St Peter's Chapel, the last half heading through the Dengie Peninsula.

- The **Three Forests Way** passes through Epping, Hainault and Hatfield forests on its 60 miles.

There are many different types of

long-distance path in Essex, as these three routes demonstrate.

- The **Colne Valley Path** keeps the river close at hand throughout its 23 miles from Great Yeldham to Colchester. Part of it coincides with the Essex Way.

- The **Flitch Way** follows the old Braintree to Bishop's Stortford railway for 15 miles. Passing through Great Dunmow, it is named for the famous 'Flitch Trials' of that town, a four-yearly examination to find the most contented married couples with local links.

- The **Saffron Trail** runs 72 miles from the pier at Southend-on-Sea through Danbury, Chelmsford and Great Dunmow to Saffron Walden. It was established by Redbridge Ramblers in 2009.

The last three walks all pass through metropolitan Essex.

- The **Hadleigh to Stratford Legacy Walk** is a 72-mile Essex Ramblers initiative linking three sites of the 2012 Olympics: the Hadleigh Farm

mountain biking site (Walk 6), the White Water centre just over the Hertfordshire boundary on the River Lea, and the main park at Stratford.

- The **London Loop** and **Capital Ring** both circle the capital: the first, close to the Greater London boundary, the second mostly within the North and South Circular roads. The last 35 of the Loop's 150 miles run from the Lea Valley through Epping and Hainault Forests before taking the Ingrebourne to a Thames-side finish at Purfleet. The 78 miles of the Ring culminate in an ingenious path through Newham, from the Olympic Park along the Victorian Greenway into modern Docklands and the Woolwich foot tunnel.

The website of the Long Distance Walkers' Association, www.ldwa.org.uk, has details of these and many others on its Long Distance Paths tab. All are mapped, and between them, there's barely a corner of the county uncovered. However, bear in mind that only a few are specifically waymarked, or have a dedicated guidebook. Maps, preferably Explorer, are essential.

APPENDIX D
Further reading

Essex is the subject of one of the great classics of English nature writing, *The Peregrine*, and features strongly in the recent writings of Robert Macfarlane, Jules Pretty and others.

JA Baker, *The Peregrine*, Collins, 2011

James Canton, *Out of Essex: Re-imagining a literary landscape*, Signal Books, 2013

Douglas Carter, *Boxted: Portrait of an English Village*, CJW Publishing, 2006

Peter Caton, *Essex Coast Walk*, Matador, 2009

David Cooke, *The Nature of Essex*, Barracuda Books, 1984

Robert Gibson, *Annals of Ashdon*, Essex Record Office, 1988

Tony Gunton, *Explore Wild Essex*, Lopinga Books, 2008

Tony Gunton, *Walk Wild Essex*, Lopinga Books, 2011

John Hunter, *The Essex Landscape*, Essex Record Office, 1999

Gerald Lucy, *Essex Rock*, Essex Rock & Mineral Society, 1999

Robert Macfarlane, *The Old Ways*, Granta, 2007

Robert Macfarlane, *The Wild Places*, Hamish Hamilton, 2012

Brian Mooney and Jon Harris, *Frontier Country: A Walk around Essex Borders*, Falconbury, 2004

Nikolaus Pevsner, *The Buildings of England: Essex*, second edition, Penguin, 1965

Jules Pretty, *This Luminous Coast*, Full Circle Editions, 2011

Oliver Rackham, *The Last Forest*, Dent, 1989

Norman Scarfe, *Essex*, Faber & Faber, 1968

In fiction, *The Essex Serpent* (Serpent's Tail, 2016) by Sarah Perry gives an atmospheric description of the Essex marshes, and in poetry *Essex Clay* (Faber & Faber, 2018) by Andrew Motion recreates the poet's early life in the county.

Finally, another Cicerone guide by Peter Aylmer, *Walking in London* (2017), contains six walks in metropolitan Essex.

LISTING OF CICERONE GUIDES

SCOTLAND
Backpacker's Britain:
  Northern Scotland
Ben Nevis and Glen Coe
Cycling in the Hebrides
Great Mountain Days in Scotland
Mountain Biking in Southern and
  Central Scotland
Mountain Biking in West and
  North West Scotland
Not the West Highland Way
Scotland
Scotland's Best Small Mountains
Scotland's Mountain Ridges
Scrambles in Lochaber
The Ayrshire and Arran Coastal
  Paths
The Border Country
The Borders Abbeys Way
The Cape Wrath Trail
The Great Glen Way
The Great Glen Way Map Booklet
The Hebridean Way
The Hebrides
The Isle of Mull
The Isle of Skye
The Skye Trail
The Southern Upland Way
The Speyside Way
The Speyside Way Map Booklet
The West Highland Way
Walking Highland Perthshire
Walking in Scotland's Far North
Walking in the Angus Glens
Walking in the Cairngorms
Walking in the Ochils, Campsie
  Fells and Lomond Hills
Walking in the Pentland Hills
Walking in the Southern Uplands
Walking in Torridon
Walking Loch Lomond and the
  Trossachs
Walking on Arran
Walking on Harris and Lewis
Walking on Rum and the Small
  Isles
Walking on the Orkney and
  Shetland Isles
Walking on Uist and Barra
Walking the Corbetts Vol 1 South
  of the Great Glen
Walking the Corbetts Vol 2 North
  of the Great Glen
Walking the Munros
  Vol 1 – Southern, Central and
  Western Highlands
Walking the Munros
  Vol 2 – Northern Highlands and
  the Cairngorms
West Highland Way Map Booklet

Winter Climbs Ben Nevis and
  Glen Coe
Winter Climbs in the Cairngorms

NORTHERN ENGLAND TRAILS
Hadrian's Wall Path
Hadrian's Wall Path Map Booklet
Pennine Way Map Booklet
The Coast to Coast Map Booklet
The Coast to Coast Walk
The Dales Way
The Dales Way Map Booklet
The Pennine Way

LAKE DISTRICT
Cycling in the Lake District
Great Mountain Days in the Lake
  District
Lake District Winter Climbs
Lake District: High Level and
  Fell Walks
Lake District: Low Level and Lake
  Walks
Mountain Biking in the Lake
  District
Outdoor Adventures with Children
  – Lake District
Scrambles in the Lake District
  – North
Scrambles in the Lake District
  – South
Short Walks in Lakeland
  Book 1: South Lakeland
Short Walks in Lakeland
  Book 2: North Lakeland
Short Walks in Lakeland
  Book 3: West Lakeland
The Cumbria Way
Tour of the Lake District
Trail and Fell Running in the Lake
  District

NORTH WEST ENGLAND
AND THE ISLE OF MAN
Cycling the Pennine Bridleway
Cycling the Way of the Roses
Isle of Man Coastal Path
The Lancashire Cycleway
The Lune Valley and Howgills
The Ribble Way
Walking in Cumbria's Eden Valley
Walking in Lancashire
Walking in the Forest of Bowland
  and Pendle
Walking on the Isle of Man
Walking on the West Pennine
  Moors
Walks in Ribble Country
Walks in Silverdale and Arnside

NORTH EAST ENGLAND,
YORKSHIRE DALES
AND PENNINES
Cycling in the Yorkshire Dales
Great Mountain Days in the
  Pennines
Mountain Biking in the Yorkshire
  Dales
South Pennine Walks
St Oswald's Way and
  St Cuthbert's Way
The Cleveland Way and the
  Yorkshire Wolds Way
The Cleveland Way Map Booklet
The North York Moors
The Reivers Way
The Teesdale Way
Trail and Fell Running in the
  Yorkshire Dales
Walking in County Durham
Walking in Northumberland
Walking in the North Pennines
Walking in the Yorkshire Dales:
  North and East
Walking in the Yorkshire Dales:
  South and West
Walks in Dales Country
Walks in the Yorkshire Dales

WALES AND WELSH BORDERS
Cycling Lôn Las Cymru
Glyndwr's Way
Great Mountain Days in
  Snowdonia
Hillwalking in Shropshire
Hillwalking in Wales – Vol 1
Hillwalking in Wales – Vol 2
Mountain Walking in Snowdonia
Offa's Dyke Map Booklet
Offa's Dyke Path
Ridges of Snowdonia
Scrambles in Snowdonia
The Ascent of Snowdon
The Ceredigion and Snowdonia
  Coast Paths
The Pembrokeshire Coast Path
Pembrokeshire Coast Path Map
  Booklet
The Severn Way
The Snowdonia Way
The Wales Coast Path
The Wye Valley Walk
Walking in Carmarthenshire
Walking in Pembrokeshire
Walking in the Forest of Dean
Walking in the South Wales
  Valleys
Walking in the Wye Valley
Walking on the Brecon Beacons
Walking on the Gower

IRELAND
The Irish Coast to Coast Walk
The Mountains of Ireland
The Wild Atlantic Way and
  Western Ireland

ITALY
Italy's Sibillini National Park
Shorter Walks in the Dolomites
Ski Touring and Snowshoeing in
  the Dolomites
The Way of St Francis
Through the Italian Alps
Trekking in the Apennines
Trekking in the Dolomites
Via Ferratas of the Italian
  Dolomites: Vol 1
Via Ferratas of the Italian
  Dolomites: Vol 2
Walking and Trekking in the Gran
  Paradiso
Walking in Abruzzo
Walking in Italy's Stelvio National
  Park
Walking in Sardinia
Walking in Sicily
Walking in the Dolomites
Walking in Tuscany
Walking in Umbria
Walking Lake Garda and Iseo
Walking on the Amalfi Coast
Walking the Italian Lakes
Walks and Treks in the Maritime
  Alps

SCANDINAVIA
Walking in Norway

EASTERN EUROPE
AND THE BALKANS
The Danube Cycleway Vol 2
The High Tatras
The Mountains of Romania
Walking in Bulgaria's National
  Parks
Walking in Hungary
Mountain Biking in Slovenia
The Islands of Croatia
The Julian Alps of Slovenia
The Mountains of Montenegro
The Peaks of the Balkans Trail
The Slovenian Mountain Trail
Walking in Croatia
Walking in Slovenia: The
  Karavanke

SPAIN AND PORTUGAL
Coastal Walks in Andalucia
Cycle Touring in Spain
Cycling the Camino de Santiago
Mountain Walking in Mallorca
Mountain Walking in Southern
Catalunya
Spain's Sendero Histórico: The
  GR1
The Andalucian Coast to Coast
  Walk
The Mountains of Nerja
The Mountains of Ronda and
  Grazalema
The Northern Caminos
The Sierras of Extremadura
Trekking in Mallorca
Walking and Trekking in the Sierra
  Nevada
Walking in Andalucia
Walking in Menorca
Walking in the Cordillera
  Cantabrica
Walking on Gran Canaria
Walking on La Gomera and El
  Hierro
Walking on La Palma
Walking on Lanzarote and
  Fuerteventura
Walking on Tenerife
Walking on the Costa Blanca
The Camino Portugués
Walking in Portugal
Walking in the Algarve
Walking on Madeira

GREECE, CYPRUS AND MALTA
The High Mountains of Crete
Trekking in Greece
Walking and Trekking in Zagori
Walking and Trekking on Corfu
Walking in Cyprus
Walking on Malta

INTERNATIONAL
CHALLENGES, COLLECTIONS
AND ACTIVITIES
Canyoning in the Alps
Europe's High Points
The Via Francigena
  Canterbury to Rome – Part 2

AFRICA
Mountaineering in the Moroccan
  High Atlas
The High Atlas
Trekking in the Atlas Mountains
Walks and Scrambles in the
  Moroccan Anti-Atlas
Kilimanjaro
Walking in the Drakensberg

ASIA
Trekking in Tajikistan
Japan's Kumano Kodo Pilgrimage
Walking and Trekking in the Japan
  Alps and Mount Fuji
Jordan – Walks, Treks, Caves,
  Climbs and Canyons
Treks and Climbs in Wadi Rum,
  Jordan
Annapurna
Everest: A Trekker's Guide
Trekking in the Himalaya
Trekking in Bhutan
Trekking in Ladakh
The Mount Kailash Trek

NORTH AMERICA
British Columbia
The John Muir Trail
The Pacific Crest Trail

SOUTH AMERICA
Aconcagua and the Southern
  Andes
Hiking and Biking Peru's Inca
  Trails
Torres del Paine

TECHNIQUES
Fastpacking
Geocaching in the UK
Indoor Climbing
Lightweight Camping
Map and Compass
Outdoor Photography
Polar Exploration
Rock Climbing
Sport Climbing
The Mountain Hut Book

MINI GUIDES
Alpine Flowers
Avalanche!
Navigation
Pocket First Aid and Wilderness
  Medicine
Snow

MOUNTAIN LITERATURE
8000 metres
A Walk in the Clouds
Abode of the Gods
Fifty Years of Adventure
The Pennine Way – the Path, the
  People, the Journey
Unjustifiable Risk?

For full information on all our
guides, and to order books and
eBooks, visit our website:
www.cicerone.co.uk.

Walking – Trekking – Mountaineering – Climbing – Cycling

Over 40 years, Cicerone have built up an outstanding collection of over 300 guides, inspiring all sorts of amazing adventures.

Every guide comes from extensive exploration and research by our expert authors, all with a passion for their subjects. They are frequently praised, endorsed and used by clubs, instructors and outdoor organisations.

All our titles can now be bought as **e-books**, **ePubs** and **Kindle** files and we also have an online magazine – **Cicerone Extra** – with features to help cyclists, climbers, walkers and trekkers choose their next adventure, at home or abroad.

Our website shows any **new information** we've had in since a book was published. Please do let us know if you find anything has changed, so that we can publish the latest details. On our **website** you'll also find great ideas and lots of detailed information about what's inside every guide and you can buy **individual routes** from many of them online.

It's easy to keep in touch with what's going on at Cicerone by getting our monthly **free e-newsletter**, which is full of offers, competitions, up-to-date information and topical articles. You can subscribe on our home page and also follow us on **Facebook** and **Twitter** or dip into our **blog**.

Cicerone – the very best guides for exploring the world.

CICERONE

Juniper House, Murley Moss, Oxenholme Road, Kendal, Cumbria LA9 7RL
Tel: 015395 62069 info@cicerone.co.uk
www.cicerone.co.uk